ANTI-SEMITISM
Imperial Germany and the Federal Republic

Ernest R. Rugenstein PhD

ANTI-SEMITISM
Imperial Germany and the Federal Republic

FICTION4ALL

A FICTION4ALL PAPERBACK

© Copyright 2020
Ernest R. Rugenstein PhD

The right of Ernest R. Rugenstein to be identified as author and channel of this work has been asserted by him in accordance with the Copyright, Designs and Patents Act 1988.

All Rights Reserved

No reproduction, copy or transmission of the publication may be made without written permission.

No paragraph of this publication may be reproduced, copied or transmitted save with the written permission of the publisher, or in accordance with the provisions of the Copyright Act 1956 (as amended).

Any person who does any unauthorised act in relation to this publication may be liable to criminal prosecution and civil claims for damages.

ISBN: 978-1-78695-483-1

This Edition
Published 2022
Fiction4All
www.fiction4all.com

Prolegomenon

The origin of this book comes from a master thesis I wrote earning my MA in European History from the University at Albany, SUNY in 2002. The original work was entitled *An Investigation into the German People's Union (Deutsche Volksunion) and a Comparison with the Christian Social Party (Christlich Sozial Partei) of Imperial Germany*. The paper examined the history and politics of the German People's Union and offered a comparison with the Christian Social (Worker's) Party and the Nazi party. It endeavored to illuminate their differences and to demonstrate that the German People's Union has greater similarity to the Nazi Party of the 1930s and 1940s than to Stöcker's Christian Social (Worker's) Party of Germany's imperial period.

The paper was reconfigured into the book you see before you with the chapters having been rearranged, revised and in cases extended. The thrust of the monograph now is anti-Semitism in Germany before and after the Nazi period and how Nazism changed how anti-Semitism was perceived socially and politically. That's not saying that some forms of anti-Semitism (or prejudice in general) is benign or that there weren't any murders, rapes and prejudicial treatment prior to the Nazi period rather a notorious ideology can become even more deadly when socio-economic situations are influx and a large number of "haves" become "have nots." Once an ideology such as anti-Semitism becomes violent and jingoistic and endemically acceptable it remains in society

The footnotes and bibliography are from the original paper. Webpages cited may not be active but can be found through the *Internet Archive Wayback Machine* (https://archive.org/web/).

Table of Contents

Prolegomenon
Table of Contents
Maps & Figures
Introduction
Definitions
Chapter 1
Background of the German Right
Chapter 2
An Anti-Semitic Party in Imperial Germany Christlich Sozial Partei/Christlich Sozial Arbeiterpartei
Chapter 3
Right-Wing Extremism in Europe and Germany During the 20th Century
Chapter 4
Anti-Semitism in the Federal Republic of Germany & The Deutsche Volksunion
Chapter 5
A Comparative Look at Anti-Semitism in the German People's Union and the Christian Social (Worker's) Party
Chapter 6
Encapsulation
Literature Review of Sources
Bibliography

Maps & Figures

Map 1: Imperial Germany 1871-191
Map 2: Weimar Republic 1918-1933
Map 3: German Reich/Greater German Reich 1933-1945
Map 4: Occupied Germany 1945-1949
Map 5: FDR & DDR 1949-1989
Map 6: Federal Republic of Germany & Länder 1989-Present3
Fig. 1: Adolf Stöcker
Fig 2: Wilhelm Marr
Fig 3: Oswald Zimmerman
Fig 4: Max Liebermann von Sonnenberg
Fig.5: Gerhard Frey
Fig 6: Otto Böckel
Fig 7: Han Ulrich Rudel
Fig 8: Joachim 'Jochen' Peiper
Fig 9: Gerhard Frey at the 1998 bayerischer DVU Convention
Fig 10: Wilfred von Oven
Fig 11: Austria's Freiheitliche Partei Österreich (Freedom Party Austria) Posters
Fig 12: Belgium's Vlaams Blok (Flemish Block) Poster
Fig 13: France's Le Front National (The National Front) Posters
Fig 14: Right-wing Newspapers
Fig 15: The Program (25 Points) of the Nazi Party

Introduction

Organized political groups can be found in nearly every international state, from multiple party systems to those with a single party. Those with multiple party systems have a flavor which is unique to the country's culture where they are found. The United States, with its enduring two-party system has major political parties with obvious policy differences and yet tend to be similar in structure. Minor parties in the US are inclined toward the extremist point of view and still, at times, reflect different facets found within the major parties. Third parties if they evolve at all have their platforms and distinctives swallowed up by one of the two major parties.

Parliamentary systems located in other parts of the world usually have a number of parties that represent the various views of the citizenry. These party perspectives include conservatives, liberals, socialists, and where legal, communist and various types of xenophobic parties. The extremist parties are usually kept from political viability either through low voter turnout or not obtaining a legislated minimum number of votes. Nevertheless, these radical parties do include a large number of constituents and at times are able to form coalitions that could command a substantial portion of the electorate. There are a number of countries in the world where this situation is demonstrated.

Germany, a federal republic with a

parliamentary government has parties elected by universal suffrage. The Parliament[1] operates by majority rule, with the Chancellor and the government drawn from the majority party or a coalition of parties. Additionally, Germany has a five per cent rule which requires a political party to win at least five per cent of the electorate before it can enter the legislature.[2]

In May 1949 when the western occupation zones were reorganizing into the new Federal Republic of Germany, they wanted to avoid the problems of the proportional representation system of the Weimar Republic. The unlimited number of parties which could gain parliamentary seats contributed to the political instability of the republic and allowed the Nazis to rise to power. To diminish this possibility in the Bundestag, and to curb the number of splinter parties which are always produced, the law designates that a party must obtain at least five per cent of the vote on the second ballot or three seats in the districts. Each of the *Länder* has similar laws which apply to their legislative elections.[3] This phenomenon of splinter political groups should not be interpreted as a new development in German history the country has a

---

[1]The lower house of parliament during the during Imperial Germany, the Weimar Republic and Nazi Germany was known as the *Reichstag*. During the Federal-Republic period it has been known as the *Bundestag*.
[2]David P. Conradt, *The German Polity* (New York: Longman, 1989), 73.
[3]Gerard Brawnthal, *Parties and Politics in Modern Germany* (Bolder, Colorado: Westview Press, 1996),46.

long history of extreme political activity.

One outcome of the revolutions throughout Europe in 1848 and specifically in Germany was the transformation of "loosely organized political groups" into viable political parties. "At the end of the revolution. . . the five principal political tendencies [were] democracy, liberalism, political Catholicism, conservatism, and workers movement(s)." Conservative strongholds were found in Prussia and in Bavaria.[4] Within these various political tendencies were found parties such as the *Wochenblatt* party, the German Democrats, and the Progressive Party. By the imperial period there were a number of political parties which had solidified their position on various issues. One of these was the Christian Social Workers Party (*Christlichsoziale Arbeiterpartei*) [CSAP] founded by the Protestant pastor Adolf Stöcker on a social reform platform. It was later renamed the Christian Social Party (*Christlichsoziale Partei*) [CSP]. Stöcker's organization was "monarchical and aristocratic" wanting a "Christian state which not only taught the virtues of obedience but inspired its rulers to take the weaker and poorer classes under their wing." Stöcker put patriotism before Liberalism and wanted the party to tap into mass support by compromising with the principles of free trade.[5] The Christian Social Party was also anti-

---

[4]Helmut Reinalter *Die deutsche Parteien vor 1918*. Cologne, 1972, translated James Chastain, February 1999, http://www.ohiou.edu/~chastain/dh/gepolpr.htm
[5]P.G.J. Pulzer, *The Rise of Political Anti-Semitism in Germany and Austria* (New York: John Wiley & Sons Inc, 1964),90-2.

Semitic, with anti-Semitism having the connotation of antagonism toward capitalism, religious Jewry, agnosticism, and marginal Christianity.

Germany at the end of the twentieth century had some 58 registered political parties, which ranged from the extreme right to the extreme left, from the Monarchists to the Communists.[6] Since the beginning of the Federal Republic of Germany a number of right-wing parties and organizations, extensively led by former Nazis or people with close ties to former Nazis, have appeared and disappeared from the political scene. Many of these parties and organizations have limited membership but very vociferous figuratively and literally.[7] Their views consist predominantly of political estrangement, xenophobia, extreme national pride, racism, and an apologetic view of Germany's Nazi past.[8]

One party which fit this pattern and began as a registered club in the early 1970s, was the *Deutsche Volksunion* (German People's Union), founded by Gerhard Frey. The DVU's party platform focused on patriotism, the exclusiveness of the German culture in Germany, support for the German military, and xenophobia. In order to avoid the

---

[6]*Political Resources on the Net - Germany*,
http://www.politicalresources.net/germany.htm
[7]Conradt, The German Polity, 73.
[8]Michael Miimkenberg, "What's Left of the Right," In Germany's New Politics: Parties and Issues in the 1990's, ed. David P. Conradt, Gerald R. Kleinfeld, George K. Romoser, and Chritian Søe, 255-271. (Providence: Berghahn Books, 1995), 266.

charge of racism and anti-Semitism, right-wing parties had substituted "culture" for "race" and "xenophobia" for "anti-Semitism."[9] The DVU's xenophobia is the thinnest of veils for the party's clear anti-Semitic drumbeat. By including other races and religions, it had merely opened the jaws of the DVU's prejudice even wider.

Those investigating right-wing extremism in Germany demonstrate continuity and draw a straight line from Wilhelm Marr, progenitor of the phrase anti-Semitism, through figures such as Otto Böckel, Max Liebermann von Sonnenberg, Oswald Zimmerman and Adolf Stöcker to National Socialism, and from there to present day right-wing, anti-Semitic extremist parties. It is common to see Stöcker portrayed as a proto-Nazi, and his party as one of the forerunners of the Nazi party. Typically, Stöcker is blamed for giving Hitler a platform and a cause to launch his crusade against the Jews.[10] Thus, the line being drawn continues through the Nazi era politics and into a number of right-wing parties which could be defined as neo-Nazi or extremist parties. The strongest of these right-wing extremist parties was the Deutsche Volksunion.[11]

---

[9]Jan - Werner Müller, *Another Country: German Intellectuals, Unification, and National Identity* (New Haven: Yale University Press, 2000), 204.
[10]Louis L. Snyder, *German Nationalism: The Tragedy of a People, Extremism Contra Liberalism in Modern German History* (Harrisburg: The Stockpole Company, 1952), 192-3. and Brawnthal, *Parties and Politics in Modern Germany* (Colorado: Westview Press), 21.
[11]Budesrepublik Deutschland, *Federal Ministry of the Interior, Press Section. Report for the Year 2000 on the Protection of*

A surface comparison between the DVU and the CSP/CSWP shows a number of apparent similarities. Both parties are portrayed as strongly nationalistic and supporting a strong centralized government. In addition, the party leaders had unquenchable thirst concerning the "imagined others" found in their midst. Stöcker railed against the Jews and those who would not support the Kaiser and the empire. He felt that non-Christians should not be put in charge over German Christians. Similarly, the DVU's platform and literature portray it as a party with a great love for German culture and history that wants Germany to be a leader in the world. Yet in its letters, newspapers, and pamphlets the DVU betrays itself as nationalistic, xenophobic, and anti-Semitic. The German government described the DVU as a neo-Nazi organization which is undemocratic, anti-Semitic in its policies and aims, and is apologetic of the Third Reich.[12] This is where the difference becomes significant between the CSP/CSWP and the DVU. With Stöcker there was a possibility of a kind of redemption. If a non-Christian German, and in some cases even unchristian non-Germans, converted to Christianity and were Germanized, they would have the same rights as any other

---

the Constitution (Köln: Bundesamt für Vefassungsschutz, 2001),
[12]Budesrepublik Deutschland, *Bundesamt für Verfassungsschutz Presse - und Öffentlichkeitsarbeit. Rechtsextremismus Parteien in der. Budesrepublik Deutschland - Agitation, Zeile, Wahlen* (Köln: Budesamt für Vefassungsschutz, 1999), 8-12.

German. Frey and the DVU cannot conceive of a political formula which transforms a non-German into a German citizen.

Often Stöcker, Hitler, and Frey are placed on a continuum, with the only real difference between Frey and Stöcker, and their respective parties, being semantics. They are both seen as working within the confines of a parliamentary system and being autocratic and anti-Semitic. The Christian Social Party and German People's Union are assumed to be Nazi style parties which bracket the Nazi period. This assumption is false: although Stöcker's party was anti-Semitic, its anti-Semitism was of a different substance than that of the DVU and the Nazis. That does not make it better, just different.

When considering this assumption, that the DVU and the Christian Social Party are of the same persuasion, and that the DVU is an extension of Stöcker's political views, it is necessary to investigate the Deutsche Volksunion's history and political distinctiveness and compare them to the Christian Social party. When analyzing Gerhard Frey's German People's Union, it will be apparent that Nazi ideology had a greater impact on the DVU than Stöcker's Christian Social Party of Germany's imperial period.

While researching the history of the DVU, CSP/CSWP, Gerhard Frey, Adolf Stöcker or comparison between them, nothing was found in English, however, there were a number of works in German. This includes works on Adolf Stöcker and his party such as Grit Koch's *Adolf Stöcker, 1835-1909: ein Leben zwischen Politik und Kirche*, which dealt with the life of Stöcker in the ministry from chaplain in the military to service as court chaplain for the Kaiser. It also considers the tension in his life between the church and politics as well as Christianity and the drives of the anti-Semitic forces at work in Germany in the latter half of the 19th century. *Protestantismus und Politik: Werk und Wirkung Adolf Stöcker by* Günter Brakelmann is another work which views this tension between the church and politics. Two other books are *Kirche am Abgrund: Adolf Stöcker und seine antijüdische Bewegung* by Hans Engelmann and *Hofprediger Adolf Stöcker und die chrislich-soziale Bewegung* by Walter Frank. These books contemplate the political and anti-Semitic side of Stöcker; however, they deal with the religious factors in his life. Frank's book, published during the Third Reich, contributed information and facts to P.J. Pulzer work, *The Rise and Fall of Political Anti-Semitism in Germany and Austria*.

Additionally, there were books on Gerhard Frey and the DVU that include *DVU im Aufwärtstrend-Gefahr für die Demokratie? Fakten, Analysen, Gegenstrategien* by Britta Obszerninks and Matthias Schmidt which deals with facts, analysis and opposition strategy of the DVU and the danger it presents to democracy. A similar book to this is *Der Multimillionär und die DVU: Daten, fakten, Hintergründe*, by Annette Link, focusing on Frey, his life, his control over the party and the party itself. Another German publication which deals with the DVU and Frey is *Braune Gefahr: DVU, NPD, REP, Geschichte und Zukuft* that is edited by Jens

Mecklenburg. Although Mecklenburg's book deals with the DVU it also discusses the NPD and REP.

Definitions

A number of definitions and abbreviations are used in this book which have various meanings in our society today. To ensure a common basis of comparison and understanding the following definitions and abbreviations will be implied when these words or letter combinations are used. The definitions which are pertinent to this study include:

Anti-Semite/Anti-Semitic - Someone who discriminates against or who is hostile toward or prejudiced against Jewish People. This includes both religious and cultural prejudice and can range from mere distaste to murderous hatred.

Conservatism -A political philosophy or attitude emphasizing respect for traditional institutions, distrust of government activism, and opposition to sudden change in the established order. During the imperial period conservative meant and deep and unrelenting commitment to the monarchy in particular and the aristocracy in general.

Liberalism - An organized political group which is not limited to, or by, established, traditional, orthodox, or authoritarian attitudes, views, or dogmas, free from bigotry. Those favoring proposals for reform, open to new ideas for progress, and tolerant of the ideas and behavior of others; broad-minded. German liberalism preferred an economic doctrine opposed to governmental regulations or interference beyond a minimum.

Progressive - A person who actively favors or strives for progress toward better conditions, as in society or government.

Right wing extremist - The people and groups who advocate the adoption of conservative and reactionary measures, especially in government and politics. Those who advocate or resort to measures beyond the norm, or the opinion of those advocating such measures.

Socialism - Those who advocate a social system in which the means of production and distribution of goods are owned collectively, and political power is exercised by the whole community.

Xenophobe - A person unduly fearful or contemptuous of that which is foreign, especially of strangers with cultural or religious differences than their own.

Abbreviations are used in this study to denote various political parties, organizations and newspapers include:

ADP - *Anti-Semitisch Deutschsoziale Partei* (Anti-Semitic German Social Party)
ADRF - *Aktion deutsches Radio und Fernsehen* (Campaign for German Radio and Television)
AEG - *Allgemeine Elektrizitätsgesellschaft*

(General Electricity Company)
AfA - *Arbeitsgemeinschaft für Arbeitsnehmerfragen* (Association of Workers)
APO - *Ausserparlamentarische Opposition* (Extra-parliamentary Opposition)
ASF - *Arbeitsgemeinschaft Sozialdemokratischer Frauen* (Association of Social Democratic Women)
AVP - *Anti-Semitische Volkspartei* (Anti-Semitic People's Party)
BBU - *Bundesverband Bürgerinitiativen für Umweltschutz* (Federal Association of Citizens Initiatives for Enviromental Security)
BdI - *Bund der Industriellen* (League of Industrialists)
BFD - *Bund Freier Demokraten* (Association of Free Democrats)
BRD/FRG - *Bundesrepublik Deutschland* (Federal Republic of Germany)
BU90 - *Bündnis 90* (Alliance 90)
BVP - *Bayerische Volkspartei* (Bavarian People's Party)
CDI - *Centralverein Deutscher Industrieller* (Central Association of German Industrialists)
CDU/CSU - *Chritslich-Demokratische Union/Christlich-Soziale Union* (Christian Democratic Union - Christian Social Union)
CSP/CSWP - *Christlich Sozial Partei/Christlich Sozial Arbeiterpartei* (Christian Social Party/Christian Social Worker's Party)
CV - *Centralverein deutscher Staatsbürger jüdischen Glaubens* (Central

Association of German Citizens of the Jewish Faith)
DA - *Demokratische Aufbruch* (Democrati Awakening)
DAF - *Deutsche Arbeitsfront* (German Labor Front)
DAP - *Deutsche Arbeiterpartei* (German Worker's Party)
DBB- *Deutsche Bauern-Bund* (German Peasants' League)
DBD - Demokratische Bauernpartei Deutschlands (Democratic Farmers Party of Germany)
DDP - *Deutsche Demokratische Partei (*German Democratic Party)
DDR/GDR - *Deutsche Demokratische Republik* (German Democratic Republic)
DFD - *Demokratischer Frauenbund Deutschlands* (Democratic Women's Association of Germany)
DFP - *Deutsche Forumpartei* (German Forum Party)
DHGV - *Deutscher Handlungs - Gehilfen Verband* (German Shop Assistant's Union)
DGB - *Deutscher Gewerkschaftbund (*German Worker's Federation)
DJ - *Demokratie Jetzt* (Democracy Now)
DK - *Deutsche Kommunistische Partei* (German Communist Party)
DKP - *Deutschkonservative Partei* (German Conservative Party)
DNVP - *Deutschnationale Volkspartei* (German National People's Party)
DR - *Deutsche Rechtspartei* (German Right Party)

DRP - *Deutsche Reichspartei* (German Reich Party)
DSU - *Deutsche Sozial Union* (German Social Union)
DSVK - *Deutsche Schutzbund für Volk und Kultur* (People's Movement for General Amnesty)
DVP - *Deutsche Volkspartei* (German People's Party)
DV - *Deutsche Volkswerein* (German People's Association)
DVU - *Deutsche Volksunion* (German People's Union)
DVU e.V. - *Deutsche Volksunion eingetragener Verein* (German People's Union registered association)
EWA - *Erster weiblicher Aufruf* (First Women's Appeal)
FDGB - *Freier Deutscher Gewerkschaftbund* (Confederation of Free German Trade Unions)
FDP - *Freie Demokratische Partei* (Free Democratic Party)
FVP - *die Fortschrittliche Volkspartei / Deutsch Forschrittpartei* (the Progressive Peoples Party / German Progressive Party)
GAL - *Grüne Alternative Liste* (Green Alternative List)
IFA - *Initiative für Ausländerbegrenzung* (Initiative for Foreign Delimination)
KPD - *Kommunistische Partei Deutschlands* (Communist Party of Germany)
LDPD - *Liberal Demokratische Partei*

Deutschlands (Liberal Democratic Party of Germany [DDR/GDR])
LDP - *Liberal Demokratische Partei* (Liberal Democratic Party)
NDPD - *National-Demokratische Partei Deutschlands* (National Democratic Party of Germany [DDR/GDR])
NLP - *Nationalliberale Partei* (National Liberal Party)
NPD - *National-Demokratische Partei Deutschlands* (National Democratic Party of Germany [BRD/FRG])
NSDAP - *Nationalsozialistische Deutsche Arbeiterpartei (*National Socialist German Workers Party [Nazi])
ÖDP - *Ökologisch-Demokratische Partei* (Ecological-Democratic Party)
PDS - *Partei des Demokratische Sozialismus* (Party of Democratic Socialism)
REP - *Republikaner* (Republican)
RP/FKP - Reichspartei / *Freikonservative Partei* (Reich Party / Free Conservative Party [Prussia])
SDP - *Sozialdemokratische Partei in der DDR* (Social Democratic Party of the GDR)
SDR - *Saxoian Deutsche Reformpartei* (German Reform Party of Saxony)
SED - *Sozialistische Einheitpartei Deutschland* (Socialist Unity Party of Germany)
SPD - *Sozialdemokratische Partei Deutschlands* (Social Democratic Party of Germany)

SR - *Soziale Reichspartei* (Social Imperial Party)
SRP - *Sozialistische Reichs Partei* (Socialist Reich Party)
UFV - *Unabhängiger Frauenverband* (Independent Women's Association)
USPD - *Unabhängige Sozialdemokratische Partei Deutschland* (Independent Social Democratic Party of Germany)
VL - *Vereinigte Links* (United Left)
VOGA - *Volksbewegung für Generalamnestie* (People's Movement for General Amnesty)
VR - *Vereinigte Rechte* (United Right)
WP - *Wirtschafspartei* (Business Party)
Center, Z - *Das Zentrum* (The Center Party)

Other abbreviations which are employed are newspapers and published pamphlets used in this work. They are presented separately because of the repeatability of letter combinations and include:

ADB - *Alldeutsche Blätter*
AKON - *Aktion Oder-Neiße* (Campaign Oder-Neiße)
AZJ - *Allgemeine Zeitung des Judentums*
AZ - *Arbeiter-Zeitung*
DA - *Deutsche Anzeiger*
DNZ - *Deutsche National-Zeitung*
DVB - *Deutsche Volksblatt*
DW - *Deutsche Worte*
DWZ - *Deutsche Wochen-Zeitung*
KZ - *Kreuzzeitung*
NDAZ - *Norddeutsche Allgemeine Zeitung*

NFP - *Neue Freie Presse*
NZ - *Neue Zeitung*

Chapter 1
Background of the German Right

Nationalistic right-wing parties have existed in Germany since the Imperial Era.[13] The historic Germany party system has been a pattern of regionally based *Milieuparteien*.[14] German parties originated in the ideologies of conservatism and liberalism dating from the 1700's. In the 1830's and 1840's political Catholicism, democratic radicalism, and socialism emerged. However, due to the long-delayed establishment of parliamentary institutions did not arise until the mid-1800's. Political parties in Imperial Germany had neither a clear religious nor clear class base except the Center Party. Political parties are best described as an assemblage of political expressions, such as social, religious and regional factors were merged into comparatively stable socio-cultural *milieus*. Most of the parties were relatively disjointed organizations whose main focus of activity lay in parliamentary bodies of the *Reich* and its constituent states.[15] The structure of

---

[13] Department of the Army, *US Army Area Handbook for Germany, Foreign Areas Studies Division: Special Operations Research*, (Washington DC, 1964), 555.
[14] *Milieuparteien* – Political parties in Germany were concerned with local and regional issues and the socioeconomic environment in which they found themselves.
[15] Karl Rohe, *Elections, Parties and Political Traditions: Social Foundations of German Parties and Party Systems, 1867-1987* (New York: Berg Publishing, 1990), 1-3, 30.

the *Reich* reflected the way it had been created and mirrored the promise rather than the achievement of the nation-state which Liberals had desired. The *Länder* (states) exercised their power in the *Bundesrat,* upper house of the Imperial Parliament, however, because Prussia had three-fifths of the total imperial population they dominated the upper house with the majority of seats. The *Reichstag*, lower house, was the more democratic element of the imperial government and far from powerless.

All imperial legislation as well as the budget needed the assent of the *Reichstag*, however, the political parties had no direct influence in the appointment of the Chancellor. This imperial position was the responsibility of the Emperor as with the respective *Länder* sovereigns over their state parliaments.[16] In general, control of the military and foreign policy was outside the purview of parliament. Further, the exclusion of parties from appointment to the government and, with some exceptions, from political patronage. Parties were not formed from struggles for power and could not offer government positions for their leaders to advance politically. The institutional separation from political obligation corresponded with the parties' deficient consciousness of responsibility and in inadequate ability to govern, integrate, and lead. Unassailable regionalism determined by differences in religion and socio-economic structure

---

[16] Peter Pulzer, *Germany 1970-1945: Politics, State Formation, and War* (New York: Oxford University Press, 1997), 18-19.

affected parties in the German *Reich*. In some cases, the ascendancy of specific political parties intensified '*Länder*' regionalism. This situation was encouraged by the electoral system which awarded an absolute majority in the election districts to the winning candidates with the effect that political parties wouldn't run a candidate where the chances of winning was hopeless.[17]

The larger German parties show their close connection with certain constituent states and regions along with certain socio-economic interest. An example of this is the German Center Party (*Deutsche Zentrumspartei*). As early as the Spring 1870 Catholics perceived a need to organize a political party to defend the interest of Catholics in North German *Länder* and Prussian legislatures.[18] The Catholic population emerged fully mobilized into politics as early as the second *Reichstag* election of 1874 with upwards of 80% of all Catholic voters casting their vote for the Center Party.[19] Other parties that were part of the *Reich* party system included *Sozialdemokratische Partei Deutschlands* (Social Democratic Party of Germany) [SPD], and the *Nationalliberalle Partei* (National Liberal Party) [NLP]. The imperial party system also spawned special interest associations such as the Deutsche Bauern-Bund (German Peasants' League) [DBB].

---

[17] Rohe, *Elections, Parties, and Political Traditions*, 30-31.
[18] Hajo Holborn, A History of Modern Germany 1840-1945 (Princeton: Princeton University Press, 1969), 259.
[19] Dieter Langewiesche, *Liberalismus in Deutschland* (Frankfort am Main: Suhrkamp Verlag, 1988), 132

The conservative parties of the empire were based on their close connection with the socially, economically, and politically dominate class of landowner in the agricultural areas east of the Elbe River in Prussia and in Mecklenburg, as well as election assistance from the Prussian administrative apparatus. This was especially true of the Deutschekonservative Partei (German Conservative Party) [DKP] which was founded in 1876 and supported the Bismarckian constitution. The party's emphasis centered on economic objectives and attracted voters from the new Prussian provinces as well as agrarian sectors of German society. Although the DKP avoided direct use of anti-Semitism many of its members were sympathetic to the anti-Semitic movements in Germany. Many conservatives believed that those who were attracted to anti-Semitic agitation and those of the working class could be won over to the conservative cause. Another political party, the CSP/CSPA, whose progeniture was Court Champlain Adolf Stöcker held an anti-Semitic agenda along with the League of German Students (*Verein Deustcher Studenten*) [VDSt] (1881),[20] which promoted anti-Semitism and nationalism in German universities.[21] An additional conservative party, which, proved important to the workings of the government was the *Reichspartei/ Freikonservative Partei* (*Reich Party/ Free Conservative Party* [Prussia]) [RP/FRP].

---

[20] *Geschicte des VDSt*, https://vdst-kiel.org/geschichte-des-vdst-kiel/
[21] Holborn, *A History of Modern Germany 1840-1945*, 266, 277, 280-283

Bismarck and his successors valued the RP/FKP as a bridge between the DKP and the NLP, both of which the RP/FKP influenced to the government's benefit.[22]

The Rise of Anti-Semitism

The Jews were extended French citizenship and basic rights by the 1791 French National Assembly. As Napoleon conquered Europe, he extended these rights to the countries whose rulers he overthrew, abolishing the system of ghettos which had been prevalent. These rights were revoked by the various German states after Napoleon's fall (1814-1815). The struggle for Jewish emancipation continued, with equal rights eventually achieved in the Netherlands and Great Britain and rights of a sort in other countries including Germany. Jews were awarded full civil rights under the constitution of the North German Federation and thereafter the Empire. In Germany and Austria, however, even after 1870 Jews were discriminated against for military and academic appointments. By the latter half of the nineteenth century emancipated Jews were becoming more noticeable in Germany's growing towns and cities. As farm laborers and peasants emigrated from rural area to urban centers, they encountered concentrations of Jewish people that were larger than where they came from.[23]

---

[22] Rohe, *Elections, Parties and Political Traditions,* 40-41.
[23] Shulamit Volkov, *The Rise of Popular Anti-Modernism in Germany: The Urban Master Artisans 1873-1896* (Princeton: Princeton University Press, 1978), 218.

Jewish people were seen as an "unpleasant novelty" to these new urban immigrants. Jews in Germany interacted with gentile society and were able to advance their socio-economic societal position. As Jewish people became more noticeable anti-Semitism became more apparent. These new immigrants to the city not only noticed the Jews but also various malcontents and demagogues who were champions of anti-Semitism. This attitude became increasing popular in the urban environment of Germany and attracted both the new immigrants and established citizens.[24] Many Germans saw the rights insisted on by Jewish people as a demand by the minority on a majority. These common Germans felt they were barely emancipated themselves and should gain their rights before the Jews.

Anti-Semitic attitudes grew among university students with these sentiments stronger in Austria than Germany. It was discovered that where German-Jewish antipathy was not escalated by hatred of various interconnected nationalities, and where stronger Liberal traditions were prevalent, anti-Semitism never became universal.[25] Still, many Germans felt the Jews were profiting on the poor and dispossessed German peasants and daily workers.

A number of individuals came to the forefront of the anti-Semitic movement, one of which was Wilhelm Marr. Marr was a frustrated malcontent

---

[24] *Ibid.*
[25] P.G.J. Pulzer, *The Rise of Political Anti-Semitism in Germany and Austria* (New York: John Wiley & Sons, 1964), 254.

journalist whose hatred of Jews grew over time and who coined the phrase anti-Semitism. He wrote a series of articles about the plight of German nationals and the effects the Jews on society as a whole and the economy in particular. Marr "claimed that Judaism was barbarous and revengeful" and of questionable morality. Marr's hatred of Jews was not based only on their creed; he hated Christians too. His hatred of the alien was directly related to their possessing distinctive characteristics. This included attacking Jewish emancipation and its consequences, one of which, Marr imagined, was Jewish control of the press in Germany.[26]

The depression of 1873 dominated the feelings of anti-Semitism which were surfacing in society. As the crash worsened, blame of the Jews for financial ills became more widespread. Many in Germany, who did not realize the world-wide consequences of the depression felt the entire situation was being manipulated by the Jews. As the economic consequences of the depression grew more intense Anti-Semitism became more pronounced in German news articles and periodicals. In 1875 extreme voices of Prussian Conservatism and the Catholic Center Party had articles printed which were explicitly anti-Semitic in content and nature.[27] In 1878 the Libertas of Vienna was the first student fraternity (*Burschenschaft*) to eject Jewish members stating

---

[26] Moshe Zimmerman, *Wilhelm Marr: The Patriarch of Anti-Semitism* (New York: Oxford University Press, 1986), 48.
[27] Pulzer, *The Rise of Political Anti-Semitism in Germany and Austria*, 88.

that Jews couldn't be regarded as Germans. "By 1890 all Burschenschaften were anti-Semitic and in 1883 the Deutsche Lesenhalla at the Technical Academy had also pronounced itself anti-Semitic."[28]

A major year in the anti-Semitic movement was 1879 when in March, Wilhelm Marr published his famous book The Victory of Judaism over Germanism (*Der Sieg des Judentums über den Germanismus*), which becomes a best seller. "Readers found in the book what Marr had not written: the incentive for a war against the Jews." The monograph itself was an "attempt at socio-cultural history of the development of Jewish hegemony in the world in general and in Germany in particular."[29] The Anti-Semitism League was founded on 26 September 1879 (*The Day of Atonement*).[30] The mission of the League was to:

> ...bring together non-Jewish Germans of all denominations, all parties and all walks of life into a common, fervent union which will strive, by setting aside all special interest and all political differences, and the greatest energy, earnestness and industry, toward one aim of saving our German fatherland from complete Judaization and to make life tolerable there for the descendants of the original inhabitants. . . to force Semites back

---

[28] *Ibid.*, 252-253
[29] Zimmerman, *Wilhelm Marr: The Patriarch of Anti-Semitism*, 78.
[30] *Ibid.*, 90

into a position corresponding with their numerical strength by liberating Germanism from oppressive weight of Jewish influence in social, political, and ecclesiastical matters, and by securing for the children of Teutons their full rights to office and dignity in the German Fatherland.[31]

Marr was not the only inspiration for the league, there were a number of others involved in the creation and its perpetuation. One of the founders was Hector de Grousillier who delivered the first two speeches at the League's meetings. Marr and de Grousillier had a major difference over the direction of the League. Marr was not only an atheist but a racist too and railed against religion in general describing himself as anti-Christian and Anti-Jewish. De Grousillier envisioned the League's stance on Judaism not as anti-racial but anti-religious. In a speech de Grousillier stated the decision to use the name Anti-Semitic League instead of Anti-Jewish League was to demonstrate the difference between Jewish Germans and those who are of the *Kahal* (community). In de Grousillier's view the membership of the *Kahal* included secular Jews, and Germans who denied their Christianity.[32] An ideological divide was created with Theodor Fritsch and Herman Lucko agreeing with Marr that the movement was racial.

---

[31] Quoted by: Pulzer, *The Rise of Political Anti-Semitism in Germany and Austria*, 51.
[32] Zimmerman, *Wilhelm Marr: The Patriarch of Anti-Semitism*, 91.

The other side which included Adolf Stöcker and Eugen Dühring agreed with de Grousillier that the difference between Jews and Christians as religious.

During this period of the Empire a number of political parties emerged which were characteristically anti-Semitic. These included the Social *Reich* Party (*Soziale Reichspartei*) headed by Ernst Henrici, the German People's Association (*Deutscher Volksverein*) organized by Max Lieberman von Sonnenberg, the German Reform Party of Saxony (*Deutsche Reformpartei Sachsen*) created by Wilhelm Pickenbach, and the CSAP by Stöcker.[33] These anti-Semitic parties formed, reformed and combined of the next twenty-years. The German Reform Party of Saxony reformed with Bernhard Förster and Max Lieberman von Sonnenberg into the German Reform Party (*Deutsche Reformpartei*). Other parties that formed or evolved at this time were the *Antisemitische Deutschsozial Partei* (Anti-Semitic German Social Party) [ADSP] led by Förster, Lieberman von Sonnenberg, and Fritsch, and the *Antisemitische Volkspartei* (Anti-Semitic People's Party) [ASVP] formed by Otto Böckel.

German anti-Semitism came to the forefront twice in this twenty-year period, 1880-1881 and 1893. The 1880-1881 period came about from economic apprehension and Bismarck's quarrel with the liberal parties. In 1893, Caprivi and the conservatives were at odds with each other, which

---

[33] Volkov, *The Rise of Popular Anti-Modernism in Germany*, 219-220.

enhanced the anti-Semitic rhetoric. What kept anti-Semitism and conservatism from establishing ties was the change in conservatism between 1892 and 1896. An example of this was the Army Bill that failed on 6 May 1893 and then passed after elections on 8 July. Caprivi introduced a bill designed to increase the size of the military and to especially increase the numbers of the draft. After its failure, he dissolved the government and called for elections. The election led to loses by the liberals, partially because conservatives adopted anti-Semitism as part of their platform for the first time. However, there were elements of the National Liberals and the Center Party that began adopting anti-Semitic learnings during this period.[34]

Anti-Semitic parties did not decline after 1900 in fact the ideology was readily incorporated into an expanding number of "political and economic interest groups, and many non-political bodies such as students' corps or athletic or mountaineering clubs."[35] Fighting among purely anti-Semitic parties for preeminence brought about the incorporation of anti-Semitic doctrine into the popular parties resulting in decreasing sectarian extremism and hateful anti-Semitic propaganda producing agreement with mild anti-Semitism.[36]

The War and the Weimar Republic

---

[34] Pulzer, *The Rise of Political Anti-Semitism in Germany and Austria*, 95, 110, 118, 303.
[35] *Ibid.*, 189.
[36] *Ibid.*

A new situation developed during the First World War with the willing ness of the SPD to defend the country. With SPD's support of the war offered the possibility of integrating the labor organizations of the state and society on the basis of equality and the dismantling hostile images which the SPD, Center Party, and others had for one another. In 1917, a majority coalition in parliament was created and built upon an Inter-party Parliamentary Committee that was made up of the SPD, Center Party and the FVP. The effectiveness of the coordinating committee, in which even the National Liberal Party took part for a period of time, was limited by internal differences both between and within the participating parties.[37] On 29 September 1918 the General Staff explained to an astonished Emperor that a cease-fire could no longer be delayed. The new Chancellor was Prince Max von Baden, his deputy and the state secretaries were drawn from three of the *Reichstag* majority parties. By 28 October 1918, the German Empire had amended its constitution, under external pressure from the United States, and became a parliamentary monarchy. On the next day, 29 October, the German Fleet was ordered to set said and fight one final battle to retrieve honor for the Empire. The crews refused and on 4 November 1918 the mutineers were in command of every ship, controlling the naval base at Kiel. They elected a council and joined forces with the worker's council

---

[37] Rohe, *Elections, Parties, and Political Traditions*, 45.

of dockyard employees.[38] The Kiel mutiny was the first in a chain of revolts that became widespread across Germany. The mutineers and other military dissidents raised the Red Flag, the only standard they could fly to evade punishment. Strikers and demonstrators could hope for reform; mutineers had to opt for revolution.[39] Worker's and soldier's councils sprung up throughout Germany with the SPD and USPD gaining control of a movement they had not initiated. The German Republic was proclaimed from balcony of the Reichstag building on 9 November 1918, by the SPD. The Kaiser has abdicated that morning and with the abdication Max von Baden regarded his mandate as Chancellor as completed and handed his office over to Friedrich Ebert of the SPD. Ebert formed a government of three SPD and three USPD members. The political liberal and conservative formations simply broke up in demoralized confusion with only the Center Party and its secured confessional roots surviving.[40] In January 1919 Germany elected a Constituent National Assembly with more than 80% of the electorate voting.[41] Meeting in Weimar, the government formed in February 1919 by the SPD, the Center Party, and the German Democratic Party (Deutsche Demokratische Partei) [DDP]. It was an alliance of middle-class liberalism, moderate working-class democracy, and organized Roman

---

[38] Pulzer, *Germany 1870-1945*, 90-91.
[39] A.J. Nichols, *Weimar and the Rise of Hitler* (Glasgow: The University Press Glasgow, 1968), 10.
[40] Pulzer, *Germany 1870-1945*, 89-91.
[41] Holborn, *A History of Modern Germany 1840-1945*, 539.

Catholics. This combination aroused anger among those associated with the previous Imperial government because they felt the least patriotic elements of the German political system had seized power. These views were reflected throughout sections of German society whose power had not disappeared. The army and later the powerful ex-servicemen's association (*Stahlheim*) were especially prone to resentment as well as university students and civil servants.[42] Right-wing parties that were monarchial faced a difficult task to participate in the Weimar Republic. Large groups, such as, the DKP, RP/FKP and the anti-Semitic parties had to change significantly to participate. The conservative, who were forced to fight for their authoritarian aims via the detested means of democracy. They were so discredited that unless they cooperated with other parties, they would risk exclusion from all major decisions. The conservatives knew they would not have a chance to build a party by themselves unless they embraced nationalism and a measure of anti-Capitalism. Therefore, they joined forces with the remnant of the CSP/CSWP and the RP/FKP founded the German National People's Party (*Deutschnationale Volkspartei*) [DNVP]. The new party was extremely different from the old DKP. The DNVP managed to cross the Prussian frontier and interest those voters of other *Länder*, as well, support the social barriers. The party was able to attract conservatives of the old empire and won a strong foothold in industry

---

[42] Nichols, *Weimar and the Rise of Hitler*, 39.

and the academic world. It retained its strongholds in the agricultural sector and to collaborate with some of the larger employee organizations such as German Shop Assistant's Union (*Deutscher Handlungs – Gehilfen Verband*) [DHGV].[43] The DNVP tried to broaden its social base by modernizing its organization and electoral campaign strategies, by expanding into large cities and embedding itself in the national milieu of the Weimar Republic, and by doing so, presenting itself as a mass party.[44] However, there were conflict within the party between those who wanted to concentrate on attacking the Republic and those who were particularly interested influencing the conduct of the government. When the party did poorly un elections, the intransigent elements gained the upper hand. After the elections of 1928, the DNVP was demoralized and short on funds. The policy switched to one of strident and unrestrained opposition to the Republic. [45]

During the First World War, a Munich locksmith, Anton Drexler, attempted to organize a party which would be both worker' and a nationalistic party. By 1919 he had founded the Germans Workers' Party (*Deutsche Arbeiterpartei*) [DAP]. In September 1919 Adolf Hitler, a political instruction officer of the German Army political department, was sent out to investigate the DAP. Intrigued by the party's platform and the possibility

---

[43] Holborn, *A History of Modern Germany 1840-1945*, 538-539.
[44] Rohe, *Elections, Parties, and Political Traditions*, 48.
[45] Nichols, *Weimar and the Rise of Hitler*, 134-135.

of gaining its leadership, Hitler joined the committee as its seventh member, in charge of propaganda and meetings. On 24 February 1920, the first mass meeting took place in the *Hofbräuhaus*. Approximately 2,000 were in attendance when Hitler announced the party's new name, National Socialist German Workers Party (Nationalsozialistische Deutsche Arbeiterpartei [NSDAP or NAZI] and proclaimed a twenty-five-point program. Hitler left the army on 1 April 1920 and made the NSDAP his full-time business. The twenty-five-point program proclamation played a modest part in propaganda of the party. The program was nationalistic, anti-Semitic, and socialistic. It demanded the union of all Germans into a greater Germany (*Groß Deutschland*) and the abrogation of the Treaties of Versailles and St. Germain. Jews were to be excluded from citizen and offices, but the program incorporated more economic than political demands. All war profits were to be appropriated and all unearned income was to be terminated. The state was to take over all trusts and share profits of large industries, communalize department stores and reorganize agriculture.[46]

The NAZI Era

In the elections of March 1933, the Nazis received 43.9% of the popular vote with 89% of the

---

[46] Holborn, *A History of Modern Germany 1840-1945*, 718-719.

electorate voting. The DNVP maintained its electoral strength; however, its leaders who hoped to rally support around the party to moderate more extreme NAZI platforms, failed in this aim. The DNVP had conducted a campaign in which here and there its spokesmen indicated certain reservations with regard to NAZI radicalism, but their platform speakers never failed to stress unity of purpose that existed between the two parties in the government. The DNVP pridefully pointed out that its 8% gave the NAZI government a bare majority of 52%. However, what should have been a crucial position in the government was little consequence which was going to abolish parliamentary government. The Nazis simply disregarded the DNVP and declared the results of the election a grand victory. Hitler's party brought the whole of social life under its control and further undermined the position of the parties. The Nazis eventually outlawed or forced the dissolution of all political parties except their own ushering in what Hitler declared as The Third-Reich (*Das Dritte Reich*)[47] The Nazis drew their power from across the social strata of society with their supporters more equally distributed among the different social and demographic categories than those of any other party. In general, the Nazis were a catch-all party of protest which united, with clearly visible differences of affinity notwithstanding, non-Jewish citizens of all religions, beliefs and social backgrounds. There were two notable exceptions, religious

---

[47] *Ibid.*, 724-735.

denominationalism and the industrial proletariat.[48]

In 1939, after annexing Austria and the Sudetenland of Czechoslovakia Hitler invaded Poland and launched six years of total war. Internally, Hitler waged war against Jews, Communists, and all social and political opposition.[49] Immediately after securing power the NAZI government began to put its anti-Semitic program into effect. German-Jews faced discrimination in stages from their exclusion from public service and university positions to the boycott of Jewish businesses and the general limitation of economic existence, while a 'Aryanization' program removed property rights and the Nuremburg Laws of 1935 saw the loss of Civil Rights and the use of Star of David being enforced. In November 1938, the pogrom known as Kristallnacht occurred when Nazis and their sympathizers destroyed Jewish businesses, burned Synagogues, and killed Jews adding force and destruction to legislative discrimination. After the invasion and occupation of Poland in September 1939 Polish Jews were being rounded up and murdered. From February 1940 onward Jews were deported from the Reich to occupied Poland.[50] Hitler's Germany finally collapsed in May 1945 as American, British, Soviet, French, and other Allied

---

[48] Rohe, *Elections, Parties, and Political Traditions*, 79-81.
[49] Geoffrey K. Roberts, *Party Politics in New Germany* (Washington: Pinter, 1997), 14.
[50] *Institute for Jewish Policy Research and American Jewish Committee,* Germany,
http://www.axt.org.uk/antisem/countries/germany.htm

forces totally destroyed the NAZI regime. The defeat brought occupation and massive uncertainty about the future of Germany as a national community, much less a political system or nation-state. Between 1945 and 1949 Germany's conquerors reduced the size of the territory dividing the remainder into four military zones of occupation. All territories acquired by the Nazis during the was between 1938-1940 was repatriated back to Austria, Czechoslovakia (Sudetenland) or French (Alsace-Lorraine) rulers. Consistent with the Yalta Agreement the allies agreed German areas east of the Oder and Neisse rivers (Oder-Neisse Line), including East Prussia and Silesia were put under 'temporary' Soviet or Polish administration, about a third of prewar Germany. The ultimate fate of these territories of these Eastern territories was to be decided with a final peace treaty between Germany and wartime Allies.[51] It should be noted that the territory taken by the Soviet Union in 1939 a part of a mutual treaty between Stalin and Hitler was never given back to Poland.

After 1945 – A New Era

By the end of 1945 political parties had been authorized by military governments in all three western occupied zones. The Western Allies

---

[51] Roberts, *Party Politics in the New Germany,* 14. In 1972 the Federal Republic of Germany ratified the treaties with the Soviet Union and Poland over these territories and in effect recognized the loss as permanent. Many right-wing extremists do not recognize this situation.

permitted nationalistic but not neo-fascist groups to organize.[52] The American, British, and French authorities allowed constitutions and parties for their zones in 1946 and 1947. The British Occupation Zone in March 1946 saw the founding of the *Deutsche Rechstpartei* (German Rights Party) [DR]. It was a result of the merger of several small right-wing parties. The horrors of the NAZI regime had no effect on a small number of citizens in Western Germany who had backed right-wing parties or action groups since 1945. The *Deutsche Reichspartei* (German Reich Party) [DRP] attracted former Nazis, especially in Lower Saxony, a which has a pro-NAZI stronghold.[53] During February 1948 the French acceded to the British-American position on the creation of a West German government. The occupational powers instructed German administrators of the *Länder* to call a constituent assembly to draft a democratic constitution which would establish a federal government structure. This was a clear indication that a federal form of government would be established with *Länder* having enough power to prevent a revival of the extreme centralization under the Nazis.[54]

The ministers-president of the *Länder*, concerned about the appearance of perpetuating the division of Germany, requested the constituent assembly be instead named the Parliamentary

---

[52] Gerard Braunthal, *Parties and Politics in Modern Germany* (Bolder, Colorado: Westview Press, 1996), 103.
[53] *Ibid.*
[54] Department of the Army, *US Army Area Handbook for Germany*, 490.

Council and the resultant document be called a Basic Law (*Grundgesetz*) rather than a constitution, emphasizing the temporary nature of the document. The council met in Bonn on 1 September, 1948 and consisted if three primary parties: *Christlich-Demokratische Union* (Christian Democratic Union) [CDU], *Sozialdemokratische Partei Deutschlands* (Social Democratic Party of Germany) [SPD], and the *Frei Demokratische Partei* (Free Democratic Party) [FDP]. These parties became known in right-wing circles as *Lizenzparteien* (licensed parties) because they had been granted permission to organize by the Allies. In the view of the right wing this meant these parties were founded as agents of the conquerors and did not represent the interests of the German people.[55]

The Parliamentary Council presented a draft of the basic Law to the Allied Military Governors in March 1949, and by May the Germans and Allies had ironed out their differences. On 8 May, the Law was ratified by the *Länder* diets except Bavaria, which objected to the amount of federal control. The Law was promulgated on 22 May 1949 and by September the organs of the *Bundesrepublik Deutschland* (Federal Republic of Germany) [BRD/FRG] were in operation. Because of the occupation status the Allies maintained the right of general supervision of German administration and

---

[55] John D. Nagle, *The National Democratic Party: Party Radicalism in the Federal Republic of Germany* (Berkeley: University of California, 1970), 16

legislation, the power to execute, decartelize, demilitarized policies, control German foreign trade and relations, and the right to preserve the position of occupational forces.[56] In the October 1949 election the DR won 1.8% of the votes and five seats in the *Bundestag*. Later in October the nationalistic majority of the DR party expelled the former Nazis within its ranks because of the influence they were amassing. On the day of the expulsion the former Nazis and the rising neo-Nazis formed the *Sozialistische Reichs Partei* (Socialist Reich Party) [SRP]. The SRP became an attraction for most radical groups especially in northern Germany.[57] The party absorbed extreme members of other right-wing groups including two *Bundestag* deputies elected on the ticket of the DR.[58] After the 1949 election cycle the BRD/FRG enacted the 5% rule for *Bundestag* elections. The election law reduced the number of splinter parties in the Bundestag and stipulated that a party must gain at least 5% of the vote on the second ballot or three seats in the voting district. Similar election laws applied in the *Länder* legislative elections.[59]

"In 1951, the SRP gained 11% of the vote in Lower Saxony and nearly 8% in Bremen"[60] A great

---

[56] Department of the Army, *US Army Area Handbook for Germany,* 490-491.
[57] Braunthal, *Parties and Politics in Modern Germany*, 104-105.
[58] Department of the Army, *US Army Area Handbook for Germany,* 564.
[59] Braunthal, *Parties and Politics in Modern Germany*, 47.
[60] *Ibid.*, 104.

deal of its support was from those who were expellees from East Prussia and Pomerania along with refugees from other eastern territories formerly inhabited by Germans. Others were ultranationalists who dreamed of a reconstructed, powerful Germany.[61] Because the SRP emulated the Nazi party the federal government appealed to the *Länder* to limit its activities and to outlaw its parliamentary units, including its strong-arm squads and its youth division.[62] "In 1952, the Constitutional Court, acting om request of the federal government, declared the party unconstitutional for its failure to support democratic government, anti-Semitism, and its authoritarian party structure.[63]

The Soviet zone of occupation in Eastern Germany also encouraged the emergence of a native political force. In the Soviet situation it would prevent a resurgence of expansionist and specifically anti-Soviet impulses of the past. As events in "West Germany" (BRD/FRG) developed the Soviets scaled down their objectives from all Germany to just the Soviet zone. In 1946 the Soviet Military Administration (SMA) forced the merger of the Social Democrats and the Communists and formed the *Sozialistische Einheitpartei Deutchland* (Socialist Unity Party of Germany) [SED]. BY 1949 the SMA was ready to proclaim the East German occupation zone as the *Deutsche Domokratische*

---

[61] *Ibid.*

[62] Department of the Army, *US Army Area Handbook for Germany,* 564.and Braunthal, *Parties and Politics in Modern Germany*, 104.

[63] *Ibid.*

Repubik (German Democratic Republic) [DDR/GDR], which was built around an effective one-party system.[64]

The Soviets allowed four other parties in addition to the SED two of which were the CDU and the *Liberal Demokratische Partei* (Liberal Democratic Party) [LDP] that had nominal counterparts in "West Germany" such as the CDU and FDP, respectively. The other two parties were the *Demokratische Bauernpartei Deutschlands* (Democratic Farmers Party of Germany) [DBD] and the *National-Demokratische Partei Deutschlands* (National Democratic Party of Germany) [NPDP] which were established by the instigation of the SED. These parties were allowed to extend the ruling party's influence in particular segments of the population. The NDPD represented the official appeal to former professional soldiers and low-level Nazis who might be brought into line with the national party. The NDPD is an exception among the secondary parties in that it increased its membership from 17,000 in 1949 to 120,000 in 1956. The Soviets formally proclaimed "East German" sovereignty in 1954.[65] The Western powers abolished the Occupational Statue in May 1955, when the Allies granted the Federal Republic of Germany full sovereignty.

During the first 15 years in the west, right-wing radicalism tended to be a taboo subject. A great deal

---

[64] Department of the Army, *US Army Area Handbook for Germany*, 573.
[65] *Ibid.*, 573, 582-583.

of debate and discussion failed to take place early on in the occupation because the great majority of people were involved in reconstruction. Reasons why the right did not grow include the rising standard of living and CDU's ability to integrate the right-wing. . . "with much greater success than any other European conservative party had achieved."[66] The CDU managed to fragment right-wing groups, at times absorbing them into the party and at other times isolating them. This left little room for a support system of explicitly right-wing and chauvinist parties.[67] By the end of 1963 it seemed clear the declining influence of the right-wing was caused by the eradication of all but the smallest right-wing sects.[68] In 1964, the right-wing was able to regroup, with an extreme-right party managing to organize a national opposition to the Bonn system of parties and exploit an anti-system mood in the context of the Bonn republic's first major economic crisis.[69] In the same year the DRP fused with other small rightist regional parties to form the *National-*

---

[66] Ulrich Wank, *The Resurgence of Right-Wing Radicalism in Germany: New Forms of an Old Phenomenon?* (New Jersey: Humanitarian Press, 1993), 73.
[67] *Ibid.*, 72-73.
[68] John D. Nagle, *The National Democratic Party: Party Radicalism, in the Federal Republic of Germany* (Berkeley: University of California, 1970), 30.
[69] Michael Miimkenberg, *"What's Left of the Right," In Germany's New Politics: Parties and Issues in the 1990's*, ed. David P Conradt, Gerald R. Kleinfeld, George K. Romoser, and Chrtian Søe, 255-271. (Providence: Berghahn Books, 1995) and Wank, *The Resurgence of Right-Wing Radicalism in Germany*, 258.

Demokratische Partei Deutschlands (National Democratic Party of Germany) [NDP][70] The party attracted people mainly from the old troubled middle class aeras which had given disproportionately high support to the Nazis during the Great Depression Additionally, many members and functionaries of the NPD had been Nazis themselves in the Third Reich.[71] In 1965 the NPD had less than 14,000 members and only acquired 2% of the vote. Even though the percentage of the vote is small it was a great achievement for a right-wing party. Many saw this apparent electoral success as a result of an ailing economy, especially in the coal and steel industries, which led to serious unemployment. Among NPD voters were disgruntled workers, self-employed, and farmers, who claimed the establishment of parties for not ending the crisis. However, in the 1970's the NPD quickly shed sway when the economy rebounded. "The NPD membership fell from 28,000 in 1969 t0 6,000 in 1982 and its electoral support shrank to less than 1%."[72]

The notion that "right-wing radicalism" would not easily pass away was confirmed through the Sinus Demographic Study of 1979-1980. The study reported 13% of the voters bore a closed, right-wing extremist view of the world, "(hatred of foreigners, of democracy, and pluralism; veneration of Volk,

---

[70] Stephen Padgett, *Parties and the Party Systemin New Germany* (Brookfield, VT: Dartmouth Publishing Co., 1993), 104
[71] Miimkenberg, *"What's Left of the Right,"* 258.
[72] Padgett, *Parties and the Party Systemin New Germany*, 105.

family, and Vaterland)," and 37% displayed biased right-wing extremist opinion. Therefore, one-half of the voters asked has either extreme right-wing views or sympathetic.[73] These outcomes were not unusual when compared to other western democracies in the 1970's and 1980's. There was a reassertion of traditional ideals of nationalism generally and especially in Germany. The rise of the new right took place in the context of social and cultural changes in Europe.[74]

The early eighties were an incubation period for the new right wing. The movements were without real intellectual influence. However, rightism gradually increased its grip on the youth. Rock bands were calling attention to themselves with acts of right-wing provocations.[75] With this third-cycle of right-wing activities the *Republikaner* (Republican) [REP].[76] The *modus operandi* of the REP was to spread fear of foreigners replacing ethnic Germans through overpopulation and destroying culture through mixing ethnicities and races. This xenophobic agitation was with racist tones by degrading human dignity. The party was successful with a simple strategy with connecting socio-economic issues as well as internal security problems being connected to immigration and in particular asylum seekers. During this same time

---

[73] Wank, *The Resurgence of Right-Wing Radicalism in Germany*, 73.
[74] Miimkenberg, *"What's Left of the Right,"* 258.
[75] Wank, *The Resurgence of Right-Wing Radicalism in Germany*, 74.
[76] Padgett, *Parties and the Party System in New Germany*, 105.

period the REP downplayed crimes of neo-Nazis by relativized them with the ongoing theme that the German people were "reeducated" by the allies after the war. Accusations of imposed and illegal constitution and placed the German Republic in question. Some could not understand why the legitimate Weimar Constitution was not reinstated. According to the REP the "West German" parliamentarianism could only be established because Germans were facing dramatized war crimes committed by Nazis the government relinquished all political self-control and consequently was helpless in resisting further "reeducation."[77] The REP presented classic right-wing agitation and was seen as the most extremist right-wing nationalistic pro-German party of the three other parties in this category. The REP had little potential of political influence, however, they attempted to mask its extreme rightist objectives and presented itself as a right-conservative party. This presented the danger that the REP would tempt democrats in good faith to vote for it.[78] By the late 1980's the REP had gained support in a number of *Länder* and claimed 20,000 members. The party's

---

[77] Bundesrepublik Deutschland, *Bundesamt für Vefassungsschutz Presse und Öffentlichkeitsarbeit. Federal Ministry of the Interior Annual Report for 1998*. (Köln: Bundesamt für Vefassungsschutz, 1999) 31-34.
[78] Bundesrepublik Deutschland, *Bundesamt für Vefassungsschutz Presse und Öffentlichkeitsarbeit. Rechtsextremismus in Deutschland – Ein Lagebild zu Beobachtungsschwerpunkten des Verfassungsschutzes* (Köln: Bundesamt für Vefassungsschutz, 2000) 12-13

greatest support came from urban, working-class districts of 18 to 24-year-old men. These young men had a minimum of education, grew-up in asocial families, living in bleak housing projects with little or none, social and cultural amenities. The party also received support from middle-class salaried employees and civil servants, including police officers who worried about their own futures or who approved of the party's law and order stance along with other conservative goals.[79]

In 1987 another right-wing party was formed the *Deutsche Volksunion-Liste D* (German People's Union or Union of German People) [DVU]. The DVU and the REP were frequently in competition for the same constituency and this relationship highlighted one problem: both were in organizational disorder.[80] At one point the two parties contemplated mutual forbearance and assistance but this led to leadership and membership problems in the REP.[81] The Munich based DVU had 25,000 members in 1989 and called for the 'Germanization' of the Germans and warned about the invasion of foreigners in the country.[82] By 2000 the DVU was the largest right-wing party in Germany with about 17,000 members.[83]

---

[79] Braunthal, *Parties and Politics in Modern Germany*, 106-107.
[80] Miimkenberg, *"What's Left of the Right,"* 267.
[81] Roberts, *Party Politics in the New Germany,* 154-155.
[82] Braunthal, *Parties and Politics in Modern Germany*, 107-108.
[83] Bundesrepublik Deutschland, *Bundesamt für Vefassungsschutz Presse und Öffentlichkeitsarbeit. Right-wing*

The Reunification of Germany

The year 1989 stood as a junction in "West German" history. A new public discourse emerged which addressed the fundamental question of national identity. The ties to neo-conservatives to the established parties had weakened to such a degree that many were ready to vote for the REP. Those who would vote for the NPD or the DVU stressed the notion that these parties had mobilized the right-wing pool which included the working class, middle class, union and nonunion voters. The parties of the right wing radicalized the neo-conservative reaction and fused its tenets with the populist anti-establishment and anti-party trust. The new right-wing of the 1990's was not simply the extension of conservatism towards the extreme right but the product of a restructuring of the political system and a regrouping of the party system.[84] It included introducing post-modern ornamentation on the old right-wing model, which constituted novel forms of political action developing from "punkers" and Fußball hooligans. The terminology 'scene' and sceneries' to describe new-right youth milieus, the role of heavy metal culture, and even the name of nightclubs such as *Richterplatz* (Judges square)

Extremism in Germany (Köln: Bundesamt für Vefassungsschutz, 2001) 12.
[84] Miimkenberg, *"What's Left of the Right,"* 259-262.

underscore this new element.[85]

Another factor of right-wing politics are organized Skinheads with the subculture scene with musical groups such as "Blood & Honor" which had been successful since the mid-1990's. The music of "Blood & Honor" represented a racist conception of the world toward national socialism and had complimentary right-wing fan magazines with circulation in the thousands and active political members in the hundreds. The German federal government believes Skinhead scene has a strong impact on youth because of the numerous right-wing music which expresses violence, racism, anti-Semitism, and an exaggerated national consciousness. The aggressive music and its provoking contents appeal to young people, especially those who feel they are socially and economically disadvantaged. This acts as an incentive for them to join the extreme right-wing political movements.[86]

Rightest renaissance in Germany was part of a pan-European upsurge of the right which began in the West and had spread to the East. In a sense, the rebirth was actually a return to normalcy for Germany. This does not mean that right-wing extremism is legitimate but merely points out the

---

[85] Michael G. Huelshott, *From Bundesrepublik to Deutschland: German Politics after Unification* (Ann Arbor: University of Michigan, 1993), 239.
[86] Bundesrepublik Deutschland, *Bundesamt für Vefassungsschutz Presse und Öffentlichkeitsarbeit. Rechtsextremismus in Deutschland – Ein Lagebild zu Beobachtungsschwerpunkten des Verfassungsschutzes*, 6-9.

fact that all modern societies call forth movements of anti-modernity. There isn't any reason why Germany be exception to this pattern.[87] Right-wing parties appropriated the concept of difference from anti-imperialist and anti-racist of the Left, setting themselves up as the defender of difference and particularity.[88] The neo-conservative culture and political elites launched efforts to define German national identity in opposition to the new Left's approach of post-national identity and "constitutional patriotism" by emphasizing the tradition of German *Kulturnation* (cultural nation) and *Völkisch* (ethnic) nationalism.[89] These parties did not feel it was necessary for Germany to sever all ties to the West but seized on unification as a new beginning and called on the nation to shed its child-like dependence on the idealized West. This meant that Germans had to overcome their supposed "fear of power" and instead normally pursue a realistically defined national interest and establish a clear scope of action.[90]

In 1990 German unification robbed the extreme right-wing of one of its central manifesto issues, however the euphoria of the East-West merger was only temporarily successful in dominating the

---

[87] Wank, *The Resurgence of Right-Wing Radicalism in Germany*, 79.
[88] Jan-Werner Müller, *Another Country: German Intellectuals, Unification, and National Identity* (New Have: Yale University Press, 2000), 203.
[89] Miimkenberg, *"What's Left of the Right,"* 260.
[90] Werner Müller, *Another Country: German Intellectuals, Unification, and National Identity,* 260.

political agenda.[91] According to a January 1993 report of the Hamburg Office for the Protection of the Constitution , there were 65,000 right-wing extremist in Germany of who 6,400 were militant and half of these right-wing militants lived in the former "East Germany."[92] Right-wing extremism and violence were often ignored in schools and in the community and many times in the eastern *Länder* the behavior wasn't even condemned. In some places in the east particularly in rural regions the slogans of the right-wing populist and extremist constitute a public consensus and acceptable way of explaining the unemployment and crime.[93] Even affluent regions in the 1990's became particularly susceptible to xenophobia. Eastern elites demonstrated considerable electoral support of right-wing extremism. Several locations in the former DDR subject immigrants to some of Europe's most dangerous violence.[94] It was apparent that the new eastern states were hardly ready to settle comfortably into "West German" democracy and there was a radicle right core of 2,000 to as many as 50,000 sympathizers.[95]

The elections to the Bundestag on 28

---

[91] Padgett, *Parties and the Party Systemin New Germany*, 106.
[92] Wank, *The Resurgence of Right-Wing Radicalism in Germany*, 76.
[93] Toralf Staud, "*Fremdenfeindlichkeit bliebt zu oft unwidersprochen: Courage-ein Schul Projekt in Sachsen*," Kulturechronik 2001 19, Nr 3 (2001), 22.
[94] Dirk Schümer, "Europa und die Fremdenfeindlichkeit
[95] Diethelm Prowe, "Prospects for the New Germany: Reading the Historical Evidence 1945-1960 and 1989 -1991," The Historian 54 (Autumn, 1991), 20.

September 1998 and the concurrent election to the *Landtag* of *Mecklenburg-Vorpommern* ended with a clear defeat for the right-wing extremist parties. Even the DVU a favorite of *Mecklenburg-Vorpommern* failed to overcome the 5% hurdle and consequently could not achieve the high expectations of the party's headquarters in Munich. The deciding factor for the poor election result of right-wing extremist parties was most probably the power-consuming rivalry between the DVU, NDP, and the REP causing fragmentation within their own camps and as far as the undecided voter was concerned scarcely creating a convincing impression. These election results, which are encouraging from a democratic point of view, should not be allowed to distract from the fact that right-wing extremist stream has stabilized in Eastern Germany with 10% of the 18 to 24-year-old in the east voting for right-wing extremist parties in the federal election. As opposed to previous decades when right-wing extremism in the west was largely the province of the older generation whereas the right-wing extremist camp in the east had a younger following.[96] At the end of the twentieth century the right-wing may be defeated and dispersed but it isn't dead.

---

[96] Bundesrepublik Deutschland, *Federal Office for the Protection of the Constitution, Trends in Right-Wing Extremism in the New Federal States*. (Köln: Bundesamt für Vefassungsschutz, 2000) 1.

Chapter 2
An Anti-Semitic Party in Imperial Germany
Christlich Sozial Partei/Christlich Sozial Arbeiterpartei

Anti-Semitism was present in Germany long before the Imperial Period, nevertheless, the most representative of this Imperial anti-Semitism is the Christlich Sozial Partei/Christlich Sozial Arbeiterpartei (Christian Social Party/Christian Social Worker's Party) [CSP/CSWP]. Most think of Nazis when they think of anti-Semitism. The Imperial period doesn't first come to mind however, many are not surprised but don't realize the continuity of anti-Semitism from the Imperial period through Nazism to the FRG in the 20th Century. Analyzing the CSP/CSWP will provide an example of an anti-Semitic party during the Imperial period

Adolf Stöcker CDU/CSU has been described as a bulwark of Christianity and as a center of rabid anti-Semitism, in reality it falls somewhere in between. Stöcker was fundamentally a monarchist and a conservative. He demanded that a Christian state be established on the ethics of obedience and duty through which the rulers would care for the lower classes with a sincere concern for the people. His anti-Semitism, however, was not racially grounded so much as it was based in religious and social principle. The CSP/CSWP's main thrust was not to destroy the Jews, but to keep them from gaining financial and political superiority over German citizens.

Stöcker and the Early Years

Adolf Stöcker was born in Halberstadt, Saxony-Anhalt, Germany (31 miles southwest of Magdeburg) on 15 December 1835. His father had been a blacksmith who joined the military and served thirty-seven years, rising to the rank of Sergeant. Later, after leaving the military, Stöcker father became a prison guard.[97]

Because of the sacrifices of his parents Stöcker was able to study theology at the universities of Halle and Berlin from 1854 to 1857. From 1857 to 1859 Adolf Stöcker was a private tutor in Neustadt, and from 1859 to 1863 he served a noble German family in Kurland. In 1863 Stöcker became the pastor at Seggerda, near Halberstadt where he stayed until 1866, when he was called to the pastorate at Hamersleben. At the beginning of the Franco-Prussian War Stöcker became an army chaplain, and by 1871 he was a divisional chaplain, stationed at Metz until 1874. Because of his exceptional patriotic fervor and military service, he was called to Berlin and attached to the cathedral with the post of court preacher (*Hofprediger*),

---

[97] P.G.J. Pulzer, *The Rise of Political Anti-Semitism in Germany and Austria* (New York: John Wiley & Sons Inc, 1964), 90. and Ökumeni Heiligen Lexikon, http://www.heiligenlexikon.de/BiographienA/ Adolf_Stoecker.html

serving from 1874 to 1891.[98]

Stöcker position at court and in the capital created a number of opportunities for him. He held favor with the Kaiser and the highest circles at court. In 1877 he became director of the City Mission of Berlin and was horrified by the extent to which the urban German population had become secularized. They were disinterested and, in some cases, acrimonious, to the "traditional values of the Prussian state." Stöcker had two great enemies, the Progressive party and the Social Democratic party, which together controlled all the political loyalties in the capital.[99] In December 1877 Stöcker joined the *Verein für Sozialpolotik*, which had been founded by Adolf Wagner in 1872. It was as a member of this society that he was introduced to some proponents of social conservatism and to some of the conservative *Kathedersozialisten* (Socialists of the Chair).[100]

Stöcker had his own ideas of how a government should be fashioned. He believed in closer contact between the social classes as well as between the church and society. Not only did he want a state which was Christian, but also one which was a constitutional monarchy. He saw the need for an emperor to inspire leadership and held the government together and a vision of the upper classes taking the weaker and poorer classes under

---

[98] *Ibid.*
[99] Pulzer, The Rise of Political Anti-Semitism, 90-91.
[100] Shulamit Volkov, *The Rise of Popular Anti-Modernism in Germany: The Urban Master Artisans, 1873-1896* (Princeton: Princeton University Press, 1978), 220.

their wing.[101]

Early in January 1878 Stöcker campaigned passionately among the workers of Berlin. Posters emerged around north Berlin advertising a meeting at the *Handwerkersaal* (Craftsmen's room) and the creation of a new party, the Christian Social Workers Party. Stöcker was not the first Protestant conservative to agitate for social reform, but he was the first to take the social gospel to the masses. The meeting at the *Handwerkersaal* was a disaster; Stöcker eloquence fell upon deaf ears. The Social Democrats crashed the meeting and took over, with Johann Most, leader of the Berlin Social Democrats, giving a long and violent denunciation of the church. By the end of the meeting a resolution was passed, by acclamation, condemning the church for doing little for the plight of the common worker. Overall, the workers were suspicious of the clergy and feared and distrusted Stöcker political enterprise. They viewed it as an attempt to neutralize them politically. The workers had learned the rhetoric of the Social Democrats "salvation lay in their own hands," nobody was going to help them but themselves. The banner of the "old forces" -- the monarchy and the church -- held meager temptation for the Berlin proletariat.[102]

The situation in the summer of 1878 changed a number of things politically. Two attempts were made on the life of the *Kaiser*. These two attempts,

---

[101] Pulzer, The Rise of Political Anti-Semitism, 90. and Ökumeni Heiligen Lexikon,
[102] Volkov, *The Rise of Popular Anti-Modernism*, 220-1. and Pulzer, *The Rise of Political Anti-Semitism*, 90-1.

three months apart, left the nation spellbound. With the first attempt Bismarck went to the Reichstag and tried to introduce a bill to outlaw the Social Democrats. The bill was rejected, however, with the second attempted assassination Bismarck dissolved the Reichstag solving his problem with the Social Democrats. The Reichstag elected in 1877 would normally not have been dissolved until 1880; therefore, with Bismarck's actions there were elections in autumn 1878.[103]

The Christian Social Workers Party ran candidates for three of Berlin's six seats and lost miserably. The Progressive Party, with 86,411 votes, gained five seats, and the Social Democrats, with 56,146 votes, took the sixth. The DKP had 12,196 votes, and the Christian Social Workers Party received 1422. The workers had rejected Stöcker propaganda and the premise of his party.[104]

Although the CSP/CSWP was rejected by the workers, it had achieved great popularity with the assorted segments of the Berlin middle class (*Mittelstand*), in particular retailers, traders, shopkeepers, small master artisans, and officials. These were voters who were loyal to church and state but were capable of having radical sentiments.[105] Stöcker believed that the CSP/CSWP could be guaranteed middle class votes only if the party stated explicitly that it would lobby for the middle class.[106] Middle class voters not only came

---

[103] *Ibid.*
[104] *Ibid.*
[105] Volkov, *The Rise of Popular Anti-Modernism*, 221.
[106] Robert Gellately, *The Politics of Economic Despair:*

with needs, but they came with ideologies, too; they were overwhelmingly anti-Semitic. As Stöcker's meetings began to fill with *Mittelstand* instead of workers, his party became an overtly anti-Semitic one. Stöcker had nothing to lose by embracing anti-Semitism, since the workers had never really supported him. On 19 September 1879 Stöcker gave a speech concerning Jews. It was entitled, "Our Demands on Modern Judaism," and it was the first speech of many Stöcker made on the subject.[107]

The Berlin Movement

Stöcker went to Breslau in March 1880 to deliver a speech on the *Handwerkerfrage* (craftsman question). The room was filled with liberals, ex-liberals, hard-core conservatives, as well as master artisans. The speech was a foretaste of what role Stöcker was to play in the political evolution of anti-Semitism. He found it important that his potential followers should have an emotional battle cry. A phrase, slogan or idea which they could rally around. Stöcker found his battle cry in anti-Semitism.[108] In 1881, with the abandonment of the workers, Stöcker changed the name of the party from the Christian Social Workers Party to the Christian Social Party.

Anti-Semitism was practiced by a number of social conservative parties and organizations. The Jewish

---

Shopkeepers and German Politics 1890-1914 (Beverly Hills: SAGE Publications, 1974), 153.
[107] Pulzer, The *Rise of Political Anti-Semitism*, 93-4.
[108] Volkov, *The Rise of Popular Anti-Modernism*, 222.

question had surfaced once or twice because of member initiatives. Stöcker found others who were promoting anti-Semitism around Berlin. He operated in the spirit of Max Lieberman von Sonnenberg, Ernst Henrici, Bernhard Förster brother-in-law to Nietzsche. These three had jointly organized the Anti-Semitic Petition, which demanded the suspension of immigration and the exclusion of Jews from public positions. Bismarck was presented the petition in April 1882. It had been signed by 225,000 persons, with the greatest number coming from northern and eastern Prussia. Württemberg and Baden contributed seven thousand, and Bavaria, nine thousand.[109]

These diverse tendencies of Berlin anti-Semitism created an umbrella association in the *Berliner Bewegung* (Berlin Movement). The organization was a half-missionary, half-political group which included Christian Socials, conservative state socialists, and a number of reformist and anti-Semitic elements. The fate of this group depended a great deal on how Bismarck viewed it. However, this did not keep Stöcker from speaking his mind about the Jewish situation. As long as Stöcker attacked yellow journalism, the radical Berlin press, or Jewish leaders of the Social Democratic Party, he was left alone. When he began to attack Bismarck's banker Gerson Bleichröder and the rest of the haute *bourgeoisie*, Stöcker rabble-rousing tactics were not appreciated. This drew a strong admonition from the Kaiser, but Bismarck

---

[109] Pulzer, The Rise of Political Anti-Semitism, 96.

saw the potential value of the group, especially the CSP/CSWP. Bismarck hoped for a tactical alliance with the anti-Semites as he combated the socialists with anti-socialist legislation and the creation of a social security system. The Chancellor decided to support both the Berlin Movement and its political agency, the Conservative Central Committee, in the 1881 elections. Four well-known anti-Semites were among the six candidates; Adolf Wagner, Lieberman von Sonnenberg, Joseph Cremer, and Adolf Stöcker.[110]

The Berlin Movement did not fare well in the 1881 election. The Progressive Party captured all six seats in the capital, but the Conservative Central Committee was victorious in obtaining more votes than the Social Democrats. Stöcker was elected on the DKP ticket at Siegen in *Westphalia*, a constituency which he represented until 1908. Even though the election was a disappointment for the CSP/CSWP, it did achieve a better performance than any other conservative group in Berlin.[111] The Berlin Movement was the first collaborative undertaking between anti-Semites and other right-wing groups.[112] Stöcker led disgruntled members of the middle class, who had been floundering politically since the crash of 1873, into the conservative circle. He was also able to acquire

---

[110] *Ibid.*, 97-8. and *The Jewish Question and Dühring*, http://www.ety.com/HRP/books online/duehring/intro.html
[111] Pulzer, *The Rise of Political Anti-Semitism*, 99.
[112] Richard S. Levy, *The Downfall of the Anti-Semitic Political Parties in Imperial Germany* (New Haven: Yale University Press, 1975), 25.

substantial endorsement from professionals and civil servants since anti-Semitism had become respectable.[113]

Bismarck was satisfied with the election of 1881. The National Liberals were wounded, and the social legislation he wanted was passed in the Reichstag without any problems. Shortly after the election Bismarck lost interest in Stöcker and the Berlin Movement. After the poor showings in the 1881 elections the anti-Semitic character of the Berlin Movement and the part assumed by nonpartisan anti-Semites was much smaller.[114] Except for the election of 1887, when the situation favored the right, the Conservative anti-Semitic bloc never improved on its 1881 results. Not once during its existence did it win a seat in the Reichstag from Berlin.[115] Even though the Berlin Movement came up with new political techniques, they were offset by a weakness which would plague succeeding anti-Semitic initiatives -- inadequate and irregular financing.[116]

The Christian Social Party

Stöcker and the CSP/CSWP lost favor, significance, and prestige after the 1881 elections. The differences the CSP/CSWP had with the other

---

[113] Pulzer, *The Rise of Political Anti-Semitism*, 99
[114] Levy, *The Downfall of the Anti-Semitic Political Parties*, 27.
[115] Pulzer, *The Rise of Political Anti-Semitism*, 99.
[116] Levy, *The Downfall of the Anti-Semitic Political Parties*, 27.

anti-Semites was in degree of tendentiousness. Most of the anti-Semitic groups were racial and saw the Jews as an alien race which could never be transformed into Germans. Stöcker and his sympathizers could see the Jewish problem dissolve with a heartfelt conversion to Christianity. With conversion Stöcker felt that society was obligated to permit the converted Jew to full participation in German life and society. As far as Bismarck was concerned, Stöcker and his party had reached the peak of their usefulness in 1881.

In 1885 Bismarck began to become wary of Stöcker because of anti-Semitic accusations concerning the Chancellor and Bleichröder. At least twice during this period Bismarck tried to get the CSP/CSWP placed under the anti-socialist laws.[117] It also became apparent to William I that he had picked the wrong person for court chaplain. The bellicose pastor was frequently involved in scandalous affairs at mass meetings, in frequent libel suits, and court intrigue.[118] In 1887 Bismarck became even more displeased with Stöcker as Prince Wilhelm, later Wilhelm II, took greater interest in him. Bismarck saw the prince falling under the sway of the court chaplain's clique and became suspicious of his own political position. When William I died and Friederich III mounted the throne, Bismarck felt his position was secure and that Stöcker was on the way out. However,

---

[117] *Ibid.*, 107.
[118] Louis L. Snyder, *German Nationalism: The Tragedy of a People, Extremism Contra Liberalism in Modern German History* (Harrisburg: The Stockpole Company, 1952),187.

Friederich III died of cancer ninety-nine days after ascending the throne, so that on 15 June 1888 Prince Wilhelm, became Emperor Wilhelm II.[119] Bismarck and Stöcker relationship with each other and with the crown changed again. By March 1890 Bismarck and Wilhelm II were at odds. The elections of January 1890 did not favor Bismarck's political outlook. Troubles began when Bismarck and the Emperor had differences of opinion on how to handle the situation.[120] Wilhelm II had assimilated the ideas of the Stöcker Conservatives. Although he was alarmed by the Social Democrats, he refused Bismarck's plan of forced suppression opting instead for Stöcker's ideas of social reforms.[121] The final straw came when Bismarck attempted to keep authority over the Prussian ministers and obstruct the unrestrained counsel between the emperor and individual ministers. Because of the emperor's recriminations Bismarck resigned on 18 March 1890.[122]

Under Wilhelm II Stöcker continued the political behavior which he had displayed with the previous emperors. The aristocracy felt he was a socialist; the workers saw him as a crony of the rich. As he lost favor at court, the Emperor wanted to

---

[119] Dr. Arthur Rosenberg, *The Birth of the German Republic 1871-1918* (New York: Russell & Russell, 1962),34-35.
[120] Hajo Holborn, *A History of Modern Germany 1840 - 1945* (Princeton: Princeton University Press, 1969), 300-301.
[121] Rosenberg, *The Birth of the German Republic 1871-1918*, 34-35.
[122] Holborn, *A History of Modern Germany 1840 - 1945*, 300-301.

dismiss him. Wilhelm II succeeded in terminating him by ignoring him at the marriage of Princess Victoria. Stöcker, understanding the situation, submitted his resignation on 5 November 1891. After his resignation he redoubled his efforts in the CSP/CSWP and during the1893 elections.[123] In December 1892, the Conservatives met in Tivoli Hall in Berlin, where Stöcker masterminded the inclusion of anti-Semitic passages in the party program. In addition, the economic section of the program contained the familiar Christian Social and Reformist claims. Two months later Stöcker was involved in the formation of the *Bund der Landwirte* (Agrarian League), which exerted political influence for the next two decades. The CSP/CSWP was still in demand in 1893; however, because Stöcker was involved in the Agrarian League, the Junker elements of the DKP began to distrust him. When in 1895 the Social Democrats instigated a scandal against Stöcker, he was forced to break with the Conservatives altogether.[124] Although Stöcker brand of politics was losing ground, the Wartburg convention of 1896 showed he stilled believed he was viable. After 1900 the parties particularly dedicated to anti-Semitism decreased in significance, while the quantity of parties and movements which embraced anti-Semitism as part of their broad philosophy increased.[125] The CSP/CSWP made a small

---

[123] Snyder, *German Nationalism*,188.
[124] *The Jewish Question and Dühring*, http://www.ety.com/HRP/books online/duehring/intro.html
[125] Pulzer, *The Rise of Political Anti-Semitism*, 125-126.

comeback in 1907, electing Stöcker and two others. Although the ex-court chaplain remained true to his non-racist brand of anti-Semitism, his doctrine was fading fast. In fact, a faction of the CSP/CSWP was changing its political orientation to cooperate with the Center Party.[126] Stöcker continued to work against the un-Christian spirit of social democracy until he died on 7 February 1909 at Gries-bei-Bozen.[127]

From 1909 to 1912, the new chairman, Franz Behrens (1872-1943) maneuvered the CSP/CSWP into closer cooperation with the Center Party. The new chairman wanted to foster the growth of international Christian trade unions as a defense against "godless Marxism." Although the Protestant unions only made up one-fifth of the membership of the Christian unions, they were extremely useful. This caused the Center Party to lend the Christian Social Party election support. Behrens' guidance seemed sufficient to lead the CSP/CSWP in a new and independent direction. However, without decisive action from the leadership of the CSP/CSWP the DKP's grip on the social party remained secure.[128] In 1917, with most of its support gone, the Christian Social Party merged with the DKP and the *Deutschvölkische Partei* to form the right-wing DNVP (*Deutschenational*

---

[126] Levy, *The Downfall of the Anti-Semitic Political Parties*, 232.
[127] Snyder, *German Nationalism,* 188.
[128] Levy, *The Downfall of the Anti-Semitic Political Parties,* 246-2477.

Volkspartei).[129]

When reviewing Imperial Ant-Semitism parties the Christian Social (Worker's) Party is an enigma. The party strove politically for "professional corporations and compulsory arbitration, old age and invalid pensions, factory legislation, restoration of usury laws, progressive taxation, and taxation of stock exchange dealings and luxuries."[130] However, it is also a fact that the party was anti-Semitic. Many of the things Stöcker said were inflammatory and prejudicial. In his view the "Jewish Problem" was not just national but international. In speeches Stöcker made remarks such as:

> But no people suffer so much under the burden of Judaism than the Germans. Our national honor, however, is not sensitive enough to fight against this evil. . . It is not enough to speak German to be a German. One can, indeed, say -- an Evangelical, or a Catholic Frenchman, Englishman or German but not a Jewish Frenchman, Englishman or German, but a French, English or German Jew.[131]

It is also true that Stöcker was instrumental in the development of the Anti-Semitic League and the expansion of anti-Semitism into the various parties both on the left and the right.

---

[129] *Christlichesoziale Partei*, Encyclopedia Judaica (Jerusalem: Keter Publishing House Jerusalem Ltd., 1972)
[130] Pulzer, *The Rise of Political Anti-Semitism*, 93.
[131] Snyder, *German Nationalism*, 195.

Although Stöcker anti-Semitism was not racial, it was politically opportunistic. When Stöcker first started, the CSP/CSWP party was not anti-Semitic at all. However, as workers refused to join or participate, Stöcker was open to recruit other groups. Those who did show an interest in the party tended to be artisans, small business owners, and low-level officials. These groups also seemed prone to anti-Semitism. Stöcker held his ground with his own brand of anti-Semitism. One of Stöcker contemporaries, de Grousillier, speaking at an Anti-Semitic League meeting, explains how anti-Semitism did not mean Jewish Germans, but those who were religious robbers and non-Jewish Germans who deny their Christianity.

Stöcker could not be like the other anti-Semites; his social position and more importantly his beliefs prevented him from emulating them. The Marxist visualizes virtue as a matter of class, the racist sees it as a matter of blood, but to a Lutheran pastor it could only be a matter of faith and grace. Stöcker, in a speech on 3 January 1881, stated, "The Christian spirit penetrates the barriers of race, and when the Israelites are baptized, they become our brothers." Not only did Stöcker feel that salvation, professed or perceived, made a Jew a good Christian; he also felt that Jews in general should not lose their emancipated status. In a speech on 27 May 1881 Stöcker said; "Emancipation is a fact, not only amongst us, but amongst all civilized nations."[132]

---

[132] Pulzer, *The Rise of Political Anti-Semitism*, 100-101.

Adolf Stöcker was certainly a German apologist and loyal to God, king and country. He was also pro-Christian and opposed to all other religions, casting him as an anti-Semite. Stöcker may have been misunderstood and misinformed, but he was not a proto-Nazi.

Map 1: Imperial Germany 1871-1918

Map 2: Weimar Republic 1918-1933

Map 3: German Reich/Greater German Reich 1933-1945

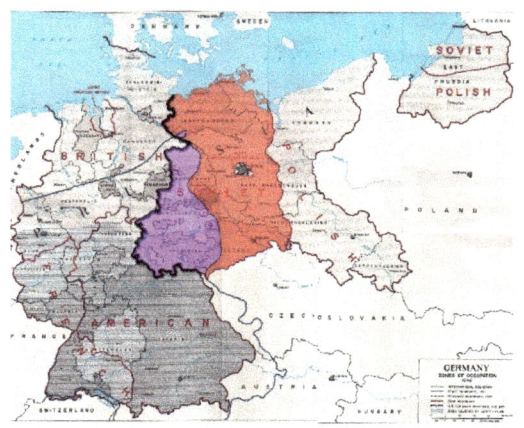
Map 4: Occupied Germany 1945-1949

Map 5: FDR & DDR (FRG & GDR) 1949-1989

Map. 6: Federal Republic of Germany & Länder 1989-Present

Fig. 1: Adolf Stöcker   Fig 2: Wilhelm Marr

Fig.3: Oswald Zimmerman   Fig. 4: Max Liebermann von Sonnenberg

Fig.5: Gerhard Frey   Fig 6: Otto Böckel

Fig 7: Hans Ulrich Rudel   Fig 8: Joachim 'Jochen' Peiper

Fig 9: Gerhard Frey at the 1998 bayerischer DVU Convention

Fig 10: Wilfred von Oven

Fig 11: Austria's Freiheitliche Partei Österreich

(Freedom Party Austria) Posters

Fig 12: Belgium's Vlaams Blok (Flemish Block) Posters

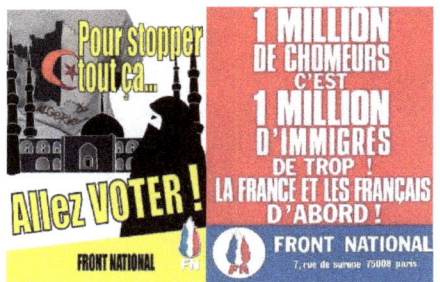

Fig 13: France's Le Front National *(The National Front) Posters*

Fig 14: Right-wing Newspapers

The Program of the German Workers' Party is a program for our time.
The leadership rejects the establishment of new aims after those set out in the Program have been achieved, for the sole purpose of making it possible for the Party to continue to exist as the result of the artificially stimulated dissatisfaction of the masses.

1. We demand the uniting of all Germans within one Greater Germany, on the basis of the right to self-determination of nations.
2. We demand equal rights for the German people (*Volk*) with respect to other nations, and the annulment of the peace treaty of Versailles and St. Germain.
3. We demand land and soil (Colonies) to feed our People and settle our excess population.
4. Only Nationals (*Volksgenossen*) can be Citizens of the State. Only persons of German blood can be Nationals, regardless of religious affiliation. No Jew can therefore be a German National.
5. Any person who is not a Citizen will be able to live in Germany only as a guest and must be subject to legislation for Aliens.
6. Only a Citizen is entitled to decide the leadership and laws of the State. We therefore demand that only Citizens may hold public office, regardless of whether it is a national, state or local office.
We oppose the corrupting parliamentary custom of making party considerations, and not character and ability, the criterion for appointments to official positions.
7. We demand that the State make it its duty to provide opportunities of employment first of all for its own Citizens. If it is not possible to maintain the entire population of the State, then foreign nationals (non-Citizens) are to be expelled from the Reich.
8. Any further immigration of non-Germans is to be prevented. We demand that all non-Germans who entered Germany after August 2, 1914, be forced to leave the Reich without delay.
9. All German Citizens must have equal rights and duties.
10. It must be the first duty of every Citizen to carry out intellectual or physical work. Individual activity must not be harmful to the public interest and must be pursued within the framework of the community and for the general good.

We therefore demand:

11. The abolition of all income obtained without labor or effort.

Breaking the Servitude of Interest.

12. In view of the tremendous sacrifices in property and blood demanded of the nation by every war, personal gain from the war must be termed a crime against the nation. We therefore demand the total confiscation of all war profits.
13. We demand the nationalization of all enterprises (already) converted into corporations (trusts).
14. We demand profit-sharing in large enterprises.
15. We demand the large-scale development of old-age pension schemes.
16. We demand the creation and maintenance of a sound middle class; the immediate communalization of the large department stores, which are to be leased at low rates to small tradesmen. We demand the most careful consideration for the owners of small businesses in orders placed by national, state, or community authorities.
17. We demand land reform in accordance with our national needs and a law for expropriation without compensation of land for public purposes. Abolition of ground rent and prevention of all speculation in land.
18. We demand ruthless battle against those who harm the common good by their activities. Persons committing base crimes against the People, usurers, profiteers, etc., are to be punished by death without regard to religion or race.
19. We demand the replacement of Roman Law, which serves a materialistic World Order, by German Law.
20. In order to make higher education – and thereby entry into leading positions – available to every able and industrious German, the State must provide a thorough restructuring of our entire public educational system. The courses of study at all educational institutions are to be adjusted to meet the requirements of practical life. Understanding of the concept of the State must be achieved through the schools (teaching of civics) at the earliest age at which it can be grasped. We demand the education at the public expense of specially gifted children of poor parents, without regard to the latter's position or occupation.
21. The State must raise the level of national health by means of mother-and-child care, the banning of juvenile labor, achievements of physical fitness through legislation for compulsory gymnastics and sports, and maximum support for all organizations providing physical training for young people.
22. We demand the abolition of hireling troops and the creation of a national army.
23. We demand laws to fight against deliberate political lies and their dissemination by the press. In order to make it possible to create a German press, we demand:
a) all editors and editorial employees of newspapers appearing in the German language must be German by race.
b) non-German newspapers require express permission from the State for their publication. They may not be printed in the German language.
c) any financial participation in a German newspaper or influence on such a paper is to be forbidden by law to non-Germans and the penalty for any breach of this law will be the closing of the newspaper in question, as well as the immediate expulsion from the Reich of the non-Germans involved. Newspapers which violate the public interest are to be banned. We demand laws against trends in art and literature which have a destructive effect on our national life, and the suppression of performances that offend against the above requirements.
24. We demand freedom for all religious denominations, provided that they do not endanger the existence of the State or offend the concepts of decency and morality of the Germanic race.
The Party as such stands for positive Christianity, without associating itself with any particular denomination. It fights against the Jewish-materialistic spirit *within* and *around* us and is convinced that a permanent revival of our nation can be achieved only from *within*, on the basis of: *Public Interest before Private Interest.*
25. To carry out all the above we demand: the creation of a strong central authority in the Reich. Unquestioned authority by the political central Parliament over the entire Reich and over its organizations in general. The establishment of trade and professional organizations to enforce the Reich basic laws in the individual states.

The Party leadership promises to take an uncompromising stand, at the cost of their own lives if need be, on the enforcement of the above points.
Munich, Germany
February 24, 1920.
Das Programm der NSDAP ("The Program of the National-Socialist German Workers' Party"); Yad Vashem
Yad Vashem - The World Holocaust Remembrance Center

Fig 15: The Program (25 Points) of the Nazi Party

Chapter 3
Right-Wing Extremism in Europe and Germany During the 20th Century

Right-wing extremism has impacted all western Europe, with many countries having been influenced by racism and xenophobia in their societies and by the corresponding organization or political party. These include parties such as France's *Le Front National* (The National Front), Austria's *Freiheitliche Partei Österreich* (Freedom Party Austria), Holland's *Centrum Partij* (Center Party), and Belgium's *Vlaams Blok* (Flemish Block) and Germany's DVU. Germany's right-wing parties range from the rabidly nationalistic to the extremist, including neo-Nazis.[133] Their presence has caused a reaction of suspicion and a demand for investigation. Governments as well as independent agencies have begun, on a yearly basis, to review these parties. Even though their political intensity is not uniform, they have in common doctrines which translate into hatred of foreigners, of asylum seekers, and those who are perceived as being outside of the race or nation.

To the outsider the different parties look very similar; it is said that only their postman can tell the

---

[133] Rinke van den Brink, "Ohne Führer kein Erfolg?" taz - LeMonde diplomatique, 15 December 1995, 7.

different right-wing party members apart.[134] However, acquiring a complete historical picture of the DVU requires a review of the party's political program and literature in English and German. It is important to see how the DVU described itself and perceived its political course in both languages. By so doing we have a tool to assist in interpreting the path the party has taken. The *Deutsche Volksunion* had a political program which details its various platforms and helps to illuminate its past. This situation highlights the importance of reviewing the findings of the government and various independent agencies. Only through such a review can a clear picture of the *Deutsche Volksunion* be obtained.

From the DVU's point of view it was neither a right-wing extremist, xenophobic, nor neo-Nazi party. The DVU pamphlets in English portray[135] it as a "Union of the German People." It claimed to be a democratic party made up of a membership which is fed up with the corrupt democratic government run by the German CDU-SPD-FDP-Greens party establishment and viewed their performance as abject failure.

The pamphlets purport that the electorate of the established parties had turned away from the election process in dismay, with almost 50% not participating at any level of German elections. The DVU demanded more referendums to allow people

---

[134] "Ob jemand Mitglied der REPs, der DVU, order der NPD geworden ist, hat nur der Briefträger zu verantworten,'"
"Würstchen ohne Senf," Der Spiegel, 7 September 1998, 48.
[135] English pamphlets and publications can be found on the internet - (Berlin: www.DVU.net/Berlin.htm, 2000)

to vote directly on political issues to restore democracy in Germany and Europe. It sought support from everyone who honestly and urgently want thing is to improve as environmental and social problems increase along with international conflicts, it asserted that the time for change was running out.[136]

The Federal Republic of Germany's Department of the Interior for the Protection of the Constitution, created to defend democracy after the ordeal of 1933-1945, annually reviews the doctrinal make-up of the various parties within the German political spectrum. The department evaluates both left and right-wing extremist groups and warns about their various idiosyncrasies. Among the parties which were regularly reviewed and investigated was the *Deutsche Volksunion*. The party disseminated the right-extremist publications with the greatest German circulation, which included the *Deutsche National-Zeitung* (DNZ) and *Deutsche Wochen-Zeitung/Deutscher Anzeiger* (DWZ/DA and *Neue Zeitung* - NZ). Because of Gerhard Frey's unrestricted leadership within the DVU, these "national-libertarian" newspapers were regarded as the publications of the Party and reflected its programmatic line and according to the government, "current affair papers" serve as a peg for continual practice of distorted presentations with the intention to agitate. Often the articles ended with advertisements for pertinent books from Frey's

---

[136] Our Aims and Principle Policies (Berlin: www.DVU.net/Berlin.htm, 2000)

publishing houses, displaying his interest in maximizing sales and profits through political agitation.[137]

The DVU was unequivocal in its pro-Europe stance. It feels that under "Globalization," Germany, on its own, is too weak to oppose the power of international banks and multinational corporations and to enforce governmental social policies for the benefit of the people. In response to this new world order, it is essential to pursue common policies with France and other European countries for the betterment of German citizens and to oppose the dictatorship of the Anglo-American bank and big business World Empire. As much as the DVU was pro-European, it was anti-imperialistic. The party supported grass roots movements in many countries which oppose "Globalization," or the "Americanization" of the world. It claimed that the new world order in the last fifty years had led to unprecedented destruction through excessive greed. There are millions of victims of poverty in "third world" countries, wars without end, and the inability of the international ruling class to create peace in the world. There was also the suggestion that the new ordering of the world had caused the destruction of the environment, which threatens the survival of humans.[138] The DVU viewed this as

---

[137] Budesrepublik Deutschland, *Bundesministerium des Innern. Annual Report of the Office for the Protection of the Constitution 1999* (Köln: Budesamt für Vefassungsschutz, 1999), 49-50.
[138] Our Aims and Principle Policies (Berlin: www.DVU.net/Berlin.htm, 2000)

proof that a new world order, the Anglo-American bank and the big business world empire, had no future despite its dictatorial power over all nations. In the coming years it would not be easy to keep Europe out of armed conflicts caused by this perishing new world order as it struggles for survival. These circumstances strengthen the rationale upon which the DVU based its call for an independent Europe.[139]

Germany's friendship with neighboring nations should not prevent it from maintaining the principle of Germany first the theme of the DVU. German firms and companies must not become prey to Anglo-American takeovers and German cities a haunt for Russian mobsters. The party was adamant in its belief that the German Army must not be used for the aims of ruthless US imperialism. Germany cannot absorb the victims of this deadly world order. Immigration of foreign professionals must not replace education of German people. The Serbs in Kosovo were cited as an example of what happens if people allow themselves to become a minority in their own country. As seen from the point of view of the DVU, among all the parties in German *Länder* parliaments, the DVU was the only one which is defending these vital interests of the German people.[140]

These beliefs and basic principles were expanded and intensified in the DVU's German publications. Three pamphlets illustrated the party

---

[139] *Ibid.*
[140] *Ibid.*

program are Deutsche Volksunion Partei-Programm (German People's Union Party – Program), Initiative für Ausländer-Begrenzung: Die überparteiliche und unabhängige Initiative für Ausländer-Begrenzung (Initiative for Foreigner-Delimitation: The Non-partisan and Independent Initiative for Foreigner- Delimitation. Action Committee for a German Germany with Just Borders) [IFA], Aktion Oder-Neiße (AKON): Aktionsgemeinschaft für ein deutsches Deutschland in gerecten Grenzen, and Jung, Deutsch, Deutlich: Was die Deutsche Volksunion für die Jugend in Deutschland erreichen will (Young, German, Clearly Understood: What the German People's Union wants to achieve for Youth.). These pamphlets were representative of published party information dealing with twelve topics which outline and define the DVU. The topics included the retention of German identity, equal rights for Germany on the world stage, protection from criminals, protection of pensions and social security benefits, the importance of the German citizen and help for middle class and farmers, direct democracy for German citizens and a number of policies which deal with family and children, job creation, youth and education, and intensified environmental and animal protection. The *Deutsche Volksunion Partei-Programm* touched on all twelve points, whereas the pamphlets Initiative für Ausländer-Begrenzung and Aktion Oder-Neiße tended to focus on their respective topics. *Jung, Deutsch, Deutlich* (Young, German, Clear) focuses on youth and the party plans for the youth culture of today. The major points of the Initiative included reformation of the system of laws, the preservation of German character, and the protection of the constitutional state. It made several declarative statements which are found in the other publications of the DVU. These mainly concern loyalty to democracy, the federal government, and the Basic Law. In addition to this was the theme "Germany is to remain German."

The case was also made for limiting the number of foreigners coming into the country. This culminates with Germany, like other nations, having the right of self-determination, a national identity, and hereditary lands. The party had no problem with those who are refugees from political persecution or who are in danger of life or limb. However, it was against those who came for economic reasons and who come because of civil war and would not return after the war is over. Further, it believed in tougher immigration laws, screening of prospective immigrants, and deportation those who did not measure up. The *Aktion* mirrors some of these points and included the undeniable German east, a German Germany, unity of all Germans, and equal rights for Germany. In the youth pamphlet (*Jung, Deutsch, Deutlich*) the DVU dealt with four basic points. These consisted of more rights for youth, the idea of Germany first, examples of workplace and educational concerns, and reasons to vote for the DVU. Each pamphlet had a declaration of the DVU's full and unreserved support for the free democratic constitutional structure of the federal government and is in full agreement with the Basic

Law.[141] Both the *Deutsche Volksunion Partei-Programm* and the DVU youth pamphlet specifically stated that the Party's political candidates, when elected into office, would take the oath that is prescribed in article 56[142] of the Basic Law.[143] The platform of the party was based on the increased stature of the German nation in the world and upon the central position of homeland, people, and family.[144]

The DVU's party platform reflects, from the governments point of view, its xenophobic ideology through one-sided and distorted reporting of abuses of political asylum and the criminal activity of foreigners. An important goal of the DVU newspapers, from the government's viewpoint, was to misrepresent and whitewash the Nazi past. With

---

[141] Grundgesetz

[142] Article 56 (Oath of Office): On assuming his office, the Federal President shall take the following oath before the assembled Members of the Bundestag and the Bundesrat: "I swear that I will dedicate my efforts to the well-being of the German people, promote their welfare, protect them from harm, uphold and defend the Basic Law and the laws of the Federation, perform my duties conscientiously and do justice to all. So, help me God." Ebner Ulm, ed., Basic Law for the Federal Republic of Germany (Berlin: German Bundestag Administration, Public Relations Section, 2001),37-8

[143] *Deutsche Volksunion Partei - Programm (München: Deutsche Vilksunion Verlag, 1999)*,1. and *Deutsche Volksunion, Jung, Deutsch, Deutlich* (Bremen: WWW.dvu.net), 2.

[144] Marco Kahlund, "DVU und Republikaner - zwei rechtsextreme Parteien im deutsche Parteiensystem" (*Staatsprüfung für die Laufban der Realschullehrer, Schleswig-Holstein,* 1999)

stereotyped headlines they foment resentment against Jews and defame representative personalities of the democratic constitutional state. The tremendous number of articles patterned on traditional right-extremist agitation demonstrated that the real concern was not to solve problems or to engage in democratic dialogue and analysis, but that sweeping opinions and defamation were to be used as a well-directed lever; the underlying ambition was for attacks against essential principles of the free democratic fundamental order.[145]

The xenophobic ideas in Frey's weekly papers were revealed in one-sided reporting about foreigners and about crimes perpetrated by foreigners. The constant employment of aggressive headlines, such as "Criminal Activity by Foreigners: Influx of Increasing Numbers of Criminals"[146] and "Do we have to let criminal foreigners stay in the country?"[147] were devised progressively and with increasing intensity to give the perception that foreigners are criminals in general. This is the voice of xenophobia. Frequently these weekly papers would apply their own editorial agenda to give slogan-like overemphasis to such generalizations.[148] It was found that the DVU effectively used stereotypes in dealing with asylum and alien

---

[145] *Bundesministerium des Innern. Annual Report of the Office for the Protection of the Constitution 1999*, 50.
[146] *Deutsche Wochen-Zeitung/Deutscher Anzeiger*, no. 6/1999, 1.
[147] Neue Zeitung, no. 38/1999, 1.
[148] *Bundesministerium des Innern. Annual Report of the Office for the Protection of the Constitution 1999*, 50.

policies. Including terms such as, "Umvolkung[149] of Germans" in their anti-foreigner articles, it tried to cause a fear of the unknown. With sensationalist headlines, such as "Germans: foreigners in their own country? The ultimate outcome of 'Multikult,'"[150] "Balkan Gypsies: hundred thousand are coming to this country! and What Germany is in for,"[151] defensive instincts were aroused and alarm about "foreignization" was instigated. Often such articles finish with advertisements for books such as *Ausländer. Die wahren Fakten* (Foreigners. The True Facts) including the hint that this new publication of the publishing house *FZ - Freiheitlicher Buch-und Zeitschriftenverlag GmBH* (also recognized as FZ-Verlag) which was founded by Frey, could be used as a trenchant weapon in any battle of words to unhinge any advocate of "foreignization" and "Multikulti."[152] Comparable concepts are based on intolerance and chauvinism. In this way it was intended to erode the inviolable principles of individual dignity and equal treatment.[153]

The government found that the DVU advocated an underlying anti-Semitism, which is prevalent

---

[149] "replacement of Germans by other nationalities"; a non-existing German word like "repeopling"
[150] multi-ethnic society; *Deutsche Wochen-Zeitung/Deutscher Anzeiger*, no. 1-2/1999, 1.
[151] *Deutsche National-Zeitung*, no. 34/1999,1.
[152] multicultural/multi-ethnic society; *Deutsche National-Zeitung*, no. 12/1999, 4.
[153] *Bundesministerium des Innern*. Annual Report of the Office for the Protection of the Constitution 1999, 50.

among right-wing extremists. In headlines and articles appearing in close succession, the weekly papers disseminated messages with anti-Semitic undertones, which propose that the German people were being prohibited by the Jews in particular from coming to terms with the German past and from joining the international community as a member enjoying equal rights. These publications alleged an over-representation of persons of Jewish faith or of Jewish ancestry in politics, trade, business, the media, and with Jewish organizations; they condemn German payments of reparations and gave polemic comments on events in Israel. While the disparaging diatribe against Jewry usually was subtly hidden between the lines, the profusion of pertinent articles clearly shows that the reader was to be made aware of a threatening influence exerted by anti-German Jews in the sense of a conspiracy theory. An article entitled "The costs we have to pay for Jews from the CIS" warned against their "mass immigration."[154]

Countless articles instigated anti-Semitic rhetoric against representatives of Jewish institutions. Examples include Ignatz Bubis, the President of the *Zentralrat der Juden in Deutschland* (Central Council of Jews in Germany) who died in August 1999, and the member of the Presidency of the Central Council of Jews in Germany, Michael Friedman.[155]

---

[154] *Deutsche Wochen-Zeitung/Deutscher Anzeiger*, no. 25/1999, 6.
[155] *Deutsche National-Zeitung,* no. 4/1999, 6.

After the death of Bubis, the DNZ and NZ carried a six-part serial, entitled "Who was Bubis really? Facts concealed from the German people," which concentrated in continuing past attacks:

> What Bubis was most concerned about, however, was to place the burden of "collective responsibility" and "collective liability" for the historical Nazi wrongs on all future generations of Germans, and to keep the German people in a state of original sin for all time to come. ... In order to have national masochism proliferate further, Bubis directed his attention to the emergence of German [nationalist] trends and parties in Germany.[156]

> Whenever the question of additional reparation payments came up, Bubis was on the spot at once. He was dead set against discontinuing payment of such tribute in the foreseeable future. ... In addition to the more than 5000 existing memorial sites for the victims of German atrocities, he kept demanding new memorials of this type to commemorate our disgrace. He wouldn't think of making such demands on Israel, the U.S. or any other country.[157]

Repeated fierce opposition to the planning and

---

[156] *Neue Zeitung*, no. 37/1999, 12
[157] *Deutsche National-Zeitung*, no. 34/1999, 3.

establishment of Holocaust memorials was rejection of an allegedly one-sided approach to coming to terms with the past. With headlines such as "The Insanity of the Holocaust Memorial,"[158] democratic politicians were accused of being obsessed by a guilt complex and of trying, with the erection of such memorials, to burden the German people with a long-term form of collective responsibility.[159]

Verification on the extent of the Holocaust was mixed by the DVU with accusations of falsification and with long debated and misrepresented facts as topical findings; the phenomenal number of victims was questioned. In this way the newspaper articles radically challenged the credibility of individual persons, and of historical reports. These articles protested different objectives of the Holocaust, and in a way evaded criminal liability- in-directly rejecting the persecution of the Jews in totality. The newspapers claimed that crucial opinions, about the historical occurrences connected with the mass murdering of Jews and other Nazi crimes, were criminalized. The following is an example of what was expressed by the party with reference to the number of victims of Nazi crimes:

> This was preceded by a nearly twenty-fold increase of the number of Auschwitz victims, i.e. to 8 million, which later was halved to four million, and then further

---

[158] *Deutsche Wochen-Zeitung/Deutscher Anzeiger*, no. 28/1999, 5.

[159] *Bundesministerium des Innern.* Annual Report of the Office for the Protection of the Constitution 1999, 51-52.

reduced to three, two, one and a half, and one million. The horrific number of "four hundred and seventy thousand to five hundred and fifty thousand" murdered Jews, given by the French- recognized-Auschwitz expert Pressac, of the *Klarsfeld-Stiftung* which certainly is above suspicion, reflects the current state of research.[160]

Repeatedly it is alleged that "Nazi hunter" Simon Wiesenthal had fabricated a photo showing Germans killed by Americans, to depict tortured and murdered concentration camp prisoners.[161]

On the occasion of the sixtieth anniversary of the outbreak of the Second World War on 1 September 1999, the DNZ and NZ, from mid-August until mid-September ran a six-part serial entitled "What led up to World War II?" Their handling of the subject implicitly gave the notion that the outbreak of the war had been part of an established plan by the United Kingdom and the US. By contrast, they claimed, Hitler had been ready to negotiate until the very last second. By reprinting public statements of the Hitler government, the DVU promoted the view of Nazi propaganda, portraying the Nazi regime as a peace-desiring victim of warmongering adversaries. These weekly papers also manipulated the public controversy concerning the traveling exhibition:

---

[160] *Deutsche National-Zeitung*, no. 30/1999, 1.
[161] Klarsfeld Foundation; *Deutsche Wochen-Zeitung/Deutscher Anzeiger*, no. 1-2/1999, 1, and *Deutsche National-Zeitung*, no. 10/1999, 1.

"War of Extermination. Crimes of the Wehrmacht, 1941 - 1944." In a myriad of articles, they presented polemics against the exhibition and rejected it as a hate and horror show[162] which abounded with manipulations and contemptible portrayals and nevertheless meandered around Germany and Austria.[163] The articles were regularly combined with advertising of the books *Die Wahrheit über die Wehrmacht. Reemtsmas Fälschungen widerlegt* and *Bilder, die fälschen. Dubiose 'Dokumente' zur Zeitgeschichte*edited (The Truth about the Wehrmacht. Reemtsma's Falsifications Refuted and Pictures that falsify. Dubious 'Documents' on Contemporary History) by Prof. Dr. Klaus Sojka, a member of the DVU National Executive Committee, and published by the FZ-Verlag.[164]

Countless articles in these newspapers agitated against what the DVU considered to be drastic and continuous demands on the State and on German companies for reparations for Jews and former forced laborers. Victims of the Nazis were attacked with aggressive headlines, such as "Paying for Hitler to the end of time - New Jewish demands for billions of deutschmark"[165] and "'Nazi-Era Forced Laborers': Playing poker for thousands of millions."[166] In addition to the criticism of the

---

[162] *Deutsche National-Zeitung*, no. 5/1999, 4.
[163] *Deutsche National-Zeitung*, no. 4/1999, 1.
[164] *Bundesministerium des Innern.* Annual Report of the Office for the Protection of the Constitution 1999, 52-3.
[165] *Deutsche National-Zeitung*, no. 30/1999, 1.
[166] *Deutsche Wochen-Zeitung/Deutscher Anzeiger*, no. 33/1999, 6.

reparation claims and of the negotiations conducted by the federal government with the victims' lawyers, it was lamented that no reparations were paid for the transgressions suffered by Germans:

> The negotiations, which have been conducted in a downright extortionist manner, about the enormous increase of German reparation payments, which anyhow have already reached astronomical amounts, threaten to end in the largest financial redistribution of all history. ... Let us recall: The Federal Republic of Germany - that is, the German taxpayer - has by now paid gigantic sums of reparations amounting to nearly 200,000 million deutschmarks. Fifty-four years after the end of the war, there is no end in sight to these expiation payments - on the contrary: ever new and higher claims are being construed. But for German victims of the victors' terror, there was, and is, no indemnification or reparation whatsoever, not even an excuse.[167]

The government found that the DVU launched polemic and defamatory attacks against the democratic constitutional state and its representatives. The aim was to divert attention from their reputation and to shake confidence in the

---

[167] *Deutsche National-Zeitung*, no. 35/1999, 1. and *Bundesministerium des Innern*. Annual Report of the Office for the Protection of the Constitution 1999, 53.

Basic Law. In particular, the DVU claimed that, for reasons of power politics, democratic politicians insisted on the common guilt of the Germans concerning the mass extermination of Jews. By doing this these "democratic politicians" intended to demoralize the nation and facilitate dominance over the people to consolidate their own power. Aberrations committed by individual politicians are generalized and constantly recalled giving the impression that all politicians and top officials are corrupt. This rhetoric is intended to promote replacing the existing State system by another system.[168]

Anti-Semitic opinions relate to reversionistic positions. Financial obligations to the Jews prompt another revisionist stance. It is regularly suggested to the readers of the DVU papers that the compensation repayments should be seen as a crime. Jewish organizations were called wirepullers because of their allegedly unparalleled agitation campaign against Austria. In addition, Holocaust memorials and payments of compensation for Nazi victims were brought up for discussion almost weekly in DVU publications. Memorials, which were described as anti-German Buß and Sühnestätten, (to atone for; atoning/conciliatory place) are represented frequently as symbols of an allegedly one-sided, anti-German world coming to terms with the past.

---

[168] *Bundesministerium des Innern.* Annual Report of the Office for the Protection of the Constitution 1999, 53-4.

In connection with the discussion about old-age pensions, the DVU defamed representatives of the democratic constitutional state as mercenary:

> It's the same as before: While impudent political bigwigs, with ever increasing emoluments and ever new benefits, continue to develop their money-raking land of milk and honey, the ordinary citizen is subjected to merciless bleeding and pillaging. The more helpless and poorer the victim, the more merciless the attacks launched by the political robber barons.[169]

Politicians' emoluments which were the subject of critical public debate provided Frey's newspapers with an opportunity to stamp Germany as a haven for political profiteers since the politicians in Bonn were record-holding money-rakers.[170]

Non-governmental agencies such as the press and anti-defamation organizations throughout Europe were finding political parties campaigning on anti-foreigner platforms and chalking up remarkable gains. Germany was found leading the way as recently published poll figures on racist attacks show.[171] As the right-wing's viewpoints in

---

[169] *Neue Zeitung*, no. 37/1999, 10.
[170] *Deutsche National-Zeitung*, no. 29/1999, 7.
[171] Mohammad A. Shaikh, "Germany Leads New Tide of Racism and Xenophobia Sweeping Europe," Muslimedia, 16-31 May 1998, Muslimedia.com.

Germany were scrutinized, extreme political views were discovered, and in some cases, unabashed Nazi sympathizers are involved. The largest of these right-wing extremist parties which has been investigated is the DVU. The party had about 15,000 active members in the country, and it was in reality so much the expression of Gerhard Frey's personal wealth that political commentators have taken to describing the DVU as Germany's "Phantom Party." A phantom possibly, but one which was winning a disquieting number of young converts.[172] DVU political candidates had been reported as being sympathetic to Hitler and the Nazis and excusing them with the explanation, "everyone makes mistakes." Others justify the Nazis with economics, saying "whatever the *Führer* and *Reichskanzler* were, they weren't pickpockets."[173] Peter Lösche, a professor of political science at Gottingen University, believes the DVU's support was drawn mainly from disaffected voters in former East German states like *Brandenburg*, where unemployment was still greater than in western Germany. Lösche said, "These are frustrated people."[174] Despite the DVU's electoral success, a study by the Konrad Adenauer Institute, which explored its behavior in the parliaments of *Bremen* and *Schleswig-Holstein* from 1987 till 1996, asserted that the party was extremely

---

[172] Charles P. Wallace, "Angry Voters Turn to the Right," Time International, 20 September 1999, 43
[173] "*Rechtsextreme Kandidaten mit Profil*," *Der Spiegel*, 7 September 1998, 48.
[174] Charles P. Wallace, "Angry Voters Turn to the Right," 43.

right wing, and its parliamentary work was "incompetent and without a political future." This portrayal was fortified in early 1999, when the DVU considered abandoning its representation in the *Sachsen-Anhalt* parliament because contention among its representatives was paralyzing its effort.[175]

The party's weekly papers, DNZ and DWZ, with a combined worldwide circulation of 60,000, spread neo-Nazi propaganda, anti-Semitism, and Holocaust denial. By the late 1990's, new subscribers received a free copy of either *KZ-Lügen* (Lies about Concentration Camps) or *Wer ist wer im Judentum* (Who's Who in Jewry). Articles which have appeared recently on the DVU's Internet website have focused on the following themes and slogans: the alleged conspiracy against Iraq; denial of Wehrmacht crimes and of German war guilt in general; *the forgotten Holocaust* -- the alleged mass murder of the German civilian population by the Allies during the war; *irredentism* -- the re-creation of a Greater Germany; *Germany for the Germans*; the potential danger of asylum seekers to German society, its economy and security; *No to the Euro! German money for the Germans!* These topics were also found in the books, videos and audio cassettes which were distributed by the DVU's *Deutscher Buchdienst*.[176]

---

[175] Steven Roth Institute for the Study of Contemporary Anti-Semitism and Race, Project for the Study of Anti-Semitism: Germany 1998-1999, Tel Aviv University, http://www.tau.ac.irl/anti-semitism/Institute.html
[176] *Ibid.*

The thrust of the Deutsche Volksunion was unquestionably focused on xenophobia, attacks against the left, a violent antipathy toward the planned European unification, and a return to Germany's "true" 1937 borders.[177] The DVU's electoral victories of the past are all the more startling since its campaigning was largely based on hate-mail and anti-foreigner posters displayed throughout the state. Normal methods of political campaigning were kept to a minimum and confined mostly to a few public appearances by Frey and a handful of his "assistants." Frey felt it wiser to rely on the hate-mail targeted on those age 18 to 29 and over 60. These DVU electoral breakthroughs were not the only manifestation of the rising tide of xenophobia in Germany. Neo-Nazis demonstrated in Leipzig on May Day 1998 in large numbers. Thousands gathered to cheer speeches calling for the deportation of foreigners who were supposedly stealing jobs from Germans and sponging off the country's welfare system.[178]

    The DVU's rhetoric stimulated large numbers of conservative supporters who are periodically dissatisfied with German politics switched their votes as a protest to the status quo. It is at these times when the DVU enjoyed its largest election returns. Even though it is explicit in its stances and positions, the DVU represents a part of Germany

---

[177] Michael G. Huelshott, *From Bundesrepublik to Deutschland: German Politics after Unification* (Ann Arbor: University of Michigan Press, 1993), 236.
[178] Mohammad A. Shaikh, "Germany Leads New Tide of Racism and Xenophobia Sweeping Europe"

which is missing. There were four elements to this appeal. First, there was an exculpation and rehabilitation of the National Socialist period. Those who lived during this time can take a certain comfort in their thoughts that as bad as it was, it was not that bad. Some may be drawn because of latent, and at times overt expressions of neo-Nazism. The second element of appeal was the invocation of traditional German values of diligence, law and order, nationalism, and anti-European Union. Third, there were those who have specific discontents, such as the size of the immigrant/foreign population or housing and other related social problems. Finally, there were those who express a general disillusionment with the established parties and their performance, a diffused protest symptomatic of the process of electoral dealignment.[179] Rightist renaissance was a consequence of the fact that traditional parties, groups, and associations had lost their cohesive force. The new, near universal shift of cultural values which had been welcomed by all sides, had also helped the extreme right.[180]

Those who looked at the *Deutsche Volksunion* with a critical eye come away with definite viewpoints. If they are generous, their findings label the DVU as merely an extreme right-wing party

---

[179] Stephen Padgett, *Parties and the Party Systems in the New Germany* (Brookfield, VT: Dartmouth Publishing Co., 1993), 92-93.
[180] Ulrich Wank, *The Resurgence of Right-Wing Radicalism in Germany: New Forms of an Old Phenomenon?* (New Jersey: Humanities Press, 1993), 80.

with overtones of ultra-nationalism and anti-foreign and asylum-seeking positions. A more critical examination would designate them as neo-Nazis, with severe nationalistic and irredentist attitudes along with anti-Semitic and anti-foreign stances. The DVU's position is encapsulated in a handbill for the 2001 city parliament election for Hamburg; *"Warum DVU wählen?"* (Why choose DVU). Reasons for supporting the DVU platform included the party's plan for an all-encompassing state investigation program which would create German workplaces for German workers, and the belief that every young person has a right to educational training. The DVU also felt that local taxes must go to the relief of Germans and to the revival of the economy. Mass immigration and dual nationality make Germans second class citizens in their own country. In addition, the party's literature argued that people should vote for the DVU because foreigners, financial asylum seekers, and so-called civil war refugees ought to be expelled, along with those who are hardened criminals. Finally, the party wants prospective voters to realize that the DVU is not a party of the affluent but is a party dedicated to helping the German people. It assumes that the old parties have failed the German people and that their government pensions should be canceled.

The DVU, from a democratic point of view, clearly had an anti-constitutional agenda. The party was under surveillance by the Office for the Protection of the Constitution and the subject of several official reports concerning its actions. Even though the government realizes that all right-wing groups draw from the same voter pool, it does not take them for granted.[181] It sees a dangerous anti-democratic party which is influencing young Germans, those who are looking for a type of patriotic pride and a history of which they could be proud. For many this is belief in a revisionist history which denies the Holocaust and the atrocities of the war. Non-government agencies had kept tabs on the DVU and come to similar conclusions. They saw a party which is controlled centrally by one man, who hates Jews, foreigners, the current state of Germany in international affairs, progressive social changes, and the loss of World War Two.

---

[181] Hans-Joachim Veen, Norbert Lepszy and Peter Mnich. *The Republikaner Party in Germany: Right-Wing Menace or Protest Catchall?* (Westport: Praeger, 1993), 1.

Chapter 4
Anti-Semitism in the Federal Republic of Germany
&
The *Deutsche Volksunion*

The history of any organization typically begins before its actual founding in the mind of its founder and the situations of society. The pattern holds true in politics, whether we look at Nazism, Bolshevik Communism, Italian Fascism, or the Democratic and Republican parties in the United States. The *Deutsche Volksunion* was no different. To investigate the history of the DVU we need to begin with the background of its principal founder Gerhard Frey and the circumstances of society.

Frey and the Early Years

Gerhard Michael Frey was born in *Cham/Oberpfalz* on 18 February 1933. He came from an old, established, business family. His father was a national conservative and had served in the *Freikorps* during the 1920's. Throughout this time Frey's father belonged to the Catholic *Bayerische Volksparte*i (BVP). His conservative attitude was stamped on the entire family with Gerhard, growing up during the Nazi reign. He went to schools influenced by Nazi doctrines and teaching a Nazi-approved curriculum. Frey inherited half of the department store chain which his father owned and today is managed by his brother, Dr. Adelbert Frey. Gerhard Frey is also a real estate buyer and owned over five hundred dwellings in Berlin, which he rented out at exorbitant rates. He was considered a slumlord by his renters, who had formed an anti-Frey committee.

In the spring of 1945 Frey witnessed the collapse of Germany, the total defeat of the German *Wehrmacht,* and the arrival of American troops. In a 1963 *Der Spiegel* interview, Frey said he wept when he saw the Fatherland struck down. Frey went on to enter an elite *Hochschule* and studied jurisprudence and political science.[182] After a period of practical and teacher training through the government of the districts of Lower Bavaria[183] he served a two-year apprenticeship with the *Passauer Neue Presse*. Frey continued his education at the University of Graz where he obtained his doctorate.[184] His dissertation was entitled *Die Handelsbeziehungen Österreichs mit Deutschland*.[185]

Beginning in the 1950's Frey strove to rehabilitate National Socialism and demonstrated that the Germans had subsequently won the Second World War. He wished to have further contact with

---

[182] Jens Mecklenburg (Hg.), Braune Gefahr: DVU, NPD, REP. Geschichte und Zukunft (Berlin: Elefanten Press, 2001), 23.
[183] Niederbayern
[184] Jörg Fischer, Ganz Rechts: Mein Leben in der DVU (Reinbek bei Hamburg: Rowolt Taschenbuch Verlag Gmbh, 1999), 70.
[185] Trade Relations Between Austria and Germany; Mecklenburg (Hg.), Braune Gefahr,23.

former prominent National Socialists. Examples would include Wilfred von Oven, propaganda specialist of the Nazi regime and a personal consultant of Goebbels, and later a close personal friend of mass murderer Adolf Eichmann. In 1951 the *Deutsche Soldaten Zeitung* (DSZ), a paper for 'brown comrades,' was founded by Waffen-SS General Paul Steiner and Frey became an employee. The DSZ was an anti-communist campaign paper in the Cold War and worked toward strengthening the relationship of former German *Wehrmacht* soldiers with the West.[186] However, as the paper's sales declined, it became financed by the United States Intelligence Service first and later from the Federal Press Office under the Adenauer government.[187] The DSZ became an important arm of propaganda by helping to win the rearmament of the *Bundesheer*.[188] and supporting the anti-communist policies of the Federal Government. In 1958 Frey purchased 50% of the shares of the DSZ-Verlag from Steiner, Helmut Damerau (ex-Nazi *Kreisleiter*), Joachim Rudolf (ex-Colonel-Waffen SS), and other old Nazis. By 1959 he had become the publisher and chief editor of the paper[189] and by 1963 Frey had become 100% owner of the paper by purchasing the remaining shares. and had changed its name from the *Deutsche Soldaten Zeitung* (DSZ)

---

[186] Ibid., 25.
[187] Annette Link, Der MultimillionŠr und die DVU: Daten, Fakten, <u>Hintergründer</u> (Essen: Klartext-Vlg., 1994), 18.
[188] Army of the Federal Republic of Germany
[189] Fischer, Ganz Rechts, 70.

to the *Deutsche National Zeitung* (DNZ).[190]

As a publisher and editor of the DNZ Frey held on to his desire to reconstruct National Socialism's history and show that the Germans had, in the long run, won the Second World War. In 1962 Gerhard Frey and Erwin Arlt co-founded an organization in Darmstadt called *Aktion Oder-Neiße* (Campaign Oder-Neiße) [AKON].[191] Others involved in the founding were publisher-director of the Deutsche National-Zeitung and CSU-official[192] Emmerich Giel, and NPD representative and past Waffen-SS Lieutenant (*Obersturmführer*), Walter Brandner.[193] The AKON saw itself as a "combat" federation for the unity of Germans and against the acknowledgment of the *Oder-Neiße* border as the western boundary of Poland. Acceptance of this boundary meant renunciation of former eastern areas of Germany such as East Prussia, Memelland, West Prussia, Danzig, Pomerania, East Brandenburg and the German-language peripheral areas of Silesia and the Sudetenland.[194] By 1963 Frey had become a spokesman for AKON, pledging the rehabilitation of National Socialism as his life's duty in an interview in *Der Spiegel*[195] Frey continued to use his publishing activities to promote the right-wing

---

[190] Mecklenburg (Hg.), Braune Gefahr, 25, 28.
[191] Britta Obszerninks and Matthias Schmidt, DVU im Aufwärtstrend - Gefahr für die Demokratic? Fakten, Analysen, Gegenstrategien (Münster: Agenda Verlag, 1998), 16.
[192] CSU-Vertiebenenfunktionär
[193] Fischer, Ganz Rechts, 12.
[194] Obszerninks and Schmidt, DVU im Aufwärtstrend, 16
[195] Mecklenburg (Hg.), *Braune Gefahr*, 23.

agenda, the furtherance of extremist views, and the rehabilitation of ex-Nazis. However, many frowned on his political views and their influence.

In 1965 fifty-seven authors and scientists, including Günter Grass and Theodor W. Adorno, demanded that the government forbid Frey's publishing activities. Fortunately for Frey the investigation was deflected because of political influence and judicial assistance from Bavarian minister Theodor Maunz. Others who stood by Frey and were counted as friends and advisors were former *Wehrmacht General* and later Chief of the Federal Security Service Reinhard Gehlen; Jurist and Bavarian Interior Minister Alfred Seid, and Federal Minister Erich Mende (FDP). Although the investigation was postponed, the subject resurfaced four years later. In 1969 Federal ministers made application under article 18[196] of the Basic Law to curtail Frey's publications and 'free' speech after the *Deutsche National-Zeitung* printed the headline "The Criminal State of Israel wants to be Our Moral Teacher." The investigation lasted for five years and by 1974 had finally withered away.[197]

A number of events occurred in 1969 which

---

[196] Article 18 (Forfeiture of Basic Rights): Whoever abuses the freedom of expression, in particular the freedom of the press, the freedom of teaching, the freedom of assembly, freedom of association, the privacy of correspondence, posts, telecommunications, the rights of property, or the right of asylum in order to combat the free democratic basic order shall forfeit these basic rights. This forfeiture and its extent shall be declared by the Federal Constitutional Court. GBL,22.
[197] Mecklenburg (Hg.), Braune Gefahr, 24.

were significant to the history of the German People's Union. In 1969 the NDP had a poor showing in the federal elections, with only 4.3%, or one and one half million votes, four hundred thousand votes short of its showing in the 1967 elections.[198] *Aktion Widerstand* (Operation Resistance) became the NDP's answer to the Ostpolitik of the new coalition. The CDU/CSU was also in opposition to the new foreign policy. For the first time in the history of the Federal Republic they found themselves as the opposition in the *Bundestag*. The new coalition in the government operated very successfully, however, eastern politics were violently disputed in the population. At a CSU party congress Franz Joseph Strauß called for the founding of a coalition movement to rescue the "*Vaterland*." The movement would unite those opposed to Ostpolitik; however, the fears of the moderate internal-party forces poisoned possibilities for a coalition.[199] Through 1970 the NPD's organized "Operation Resistance" against the Federal Government's Ostpolitik remained unsuccessful and created a deep internal crisis suggesting the party's decay. In January 1971 things began to change for the right-wing.

The Deutsche Volksunion

On the eve of the hundred-year anniversary of the Bismarckian Reich, 16 January 1971, Erwin Arlt

---

[198] Mecklenburg (Hg.), Braune Gefahr, 12.
[199] Obszerninks and Schmidt, DVU im Aufwärtstrend, 11.

and Gerhard Frey initiated the founding of the *Deutscher Volksunion eingetragener Verein* (German People's Union registered association) (DVU e.V.). Others who attended the meeting at Hotel Deutsche Kaiser, Munich, included author William Pleyer, former Waffen-SS and NPD member Walter Brandner, CSU-politician and functionary for the Germans driven from the eastern provinces Emmerich Giel, and Werner Novak, CDU member from Baden-Württemberg.[200] The Union was to be a coalition movement of national conservatives, and the extreme right-wing was to include not only the NDP but the right-wing circle of the CDU/CSU. The *Verein* (society) was not meant to be a political party but an entity for preserving conservative German politics. The DVU e.V. elected Frey as Chairman, and he immediately became the chief spokesman for the organization. In February 1971 Frey wrote in the *Deutsche Anzeiger,* "The last cause for the establishment (DVU e.V.) was the increasing surrender policy of the red government in relation to the east in their special agreements with Moscow and Warsaw. . . The DVU is not a party. It wants to unite all constitutionally faithful forces from the center to those on the right."[201] Later that year Frey bought

---

[200] *Ibid.*, 12.
[201] Letzter Anlaß für die Gründung war die sich steigernde Kapitulationspolitik der roten Regierung gegenüber dem Osten insbesonderer die Vertüage von Moskau und Warschau . . . Die DVU ist keine Partei. Sie will alle verfassungstreuen Kräfte von mitte bis rechts zusammenführen. Mecklenburg (Hg.), Braune Gefahr, 12.

the *Deutsche Anzeiger* and added it to his growing publishing empire.[202]

The DVU e.V. held its first official, and controversial, event on 3 April 1971 in Munich. Its focus was the ratification of the Eastern agreements between West Germany and the Soviet Union and Poland. Frey held to his stance that Germany had won the Second World War in a political sense, not because the desires of National Socialist war aims were achieved, but because the desires, rights, and freedoms of the German people were achieved. He promised that the agreements would never be tolerated and the purpose of the DVU e.V. was to stiffen the back of the CDU/CSU or give them a backbone. Frey organized the event under the banners "*Abrechnung mit Brandt*" and "*Kampf dem Verrat.*"[203] In the same month Frey organized a march on Bonn, with a key address being given to over 5,000 attendees.[204] Beginning with the NDP's disastrous election results of 1969, their support continued to drop through 1970 and 1971. This decline triggered right extremists to flock to the DVU e.V. so that by 1972 the union had become a collecting point for national conservatives and the voice of right-wing extremism. It established various initiatives and collaborative movements such as the Liberal Advice (*Freiheitliche Rat*),[205] initiated by Gerhard Frey in January 1972 as a coordination center for national-liberal rights. A

---

[202] Fischer, Ganz Rechts, 70.
[203] "Reckoning with Brandt" and "Struggle Against Betrayal"
[204] Mecklenburg (Hg.), Braune Gefahr, 13.
[205] *Ibid.*

network consisting of DVU e.V., Aktion Oder-Neiße, the Deutsche Block, the Jugendbund Adler, the Stahlhelm, the Arbeitskreis Volkstreuer Verbände, and the Wiking-Jungen coalesced, all of which called for Gerhard Frey to be the chairman. The aim was the manipulation of the statute of limitations on war crimes, in conjunction with a general amnesty for direct and indirect political offenses prior to 1945. In April 1972, the Freiheitliche Rat organized a march on Bonn which turned into a large demonstration with several thousand taking part. However, by 1973 the various network members were beginning to dissipate, with Frey keeping political dominance over the issues.[206]

Frey joined the NPD in 1975 and, as a member, ran for chairperson. Although not victorious, he did become a committee member on the federal board. The same year, as head of the DVU e.V., Frey outlined several political objectives through campaign programs (*Aktionsprogrammen*). These programs included agitation for stronger laws against crimes such as murder, drug trafficking, kidnapping, rape, robbery, treason, and separatism. Putting these programs to the test, Frey organized a demonstration with the slogan "Justice for German Heroes." The symbolic figures of controversy Frey put forward were French war criminal and formerly condemned *SS-Standartenführer* (SS Colonel) Jochen Peiper and decorated war hero *Luftwaffe Oberst* (Air Force Colonel) Hans Ulrich-Rudel. In December 1944 Peiper had been the *Chef SS-*

---

[206] Obszerninks and Schmidt, DVU im Aufwärtstrend, 11.

Kampfgruppe near Malmedy, where seventy unarmed US POW's were murdered. Rudel had been a Stuka dive bomber pilot, highly decorated and a glowing admirer of Adolf Hitler. Frey wrote in the *Deutsche National-Zeitung* that young men were asking for examples to emulate. Numerous models, he wrote, could be found in the German armed forces of the Second World War, instances of enormous manly (German) courage and demonstrations of duty. Frey tried to revise the populace's opinion of the German soldier and the operations which Hitler's armies carried out.

Simultaneously, Frey attempted to create National Socialist heroes.[207] An example can be found among the contributions to the *Deutsche National-Zeitung*. In 1977 Wilfred von Oven, a Nazi propagandist, wrote for the *Deutsche National-Zeitung* and praised the friendly contact and working relationship he had with Gerhard Frey. Throughout the piece von Oven used the vocabulary of the "master race" and the process of poison pill propaganda and its devastating consequences to lash out at overseas volunteers[208] who helped blacks in Africa "to have more children." Not only did the *Deutsche National-Zeitung* print quasi-racist and neo-Nazi articles, but it also dabbled in the occult. In 1977 the paper printed Frey's horoscope, which stated that he would reform a national movement and a revolution. It was written that he would be a man of enthusiasm who would fulfill his life's duty.

---

[207] Mecklenburg (Hg.), Braune Gefahr, 13.
[208] e.g. Peace Corp Volunteers

From that point on, Frey realized his life's ambition and his popularity as a publicist and publisher. His goal now was to create a program which would whitewash the German *Wehrmacht* and old Nazis, covering their past and making them look good to others.[209]

Beginning in 1979 and lasting through the 1980's, the DVU e.V. campaign communities (*Aktiongemeinschafte*) were integrated for closer cooperation after previously being independent.[210] These communities covered a wide variety of situations and included such organizations as the "People's Movement for General Amnesty" (*Volksbewegung für Generalamnestie*) [VOGA], "Campaign for German Radio and Television" (*Aktion deutsches Radio und Fernsehen*) [ADRF], and "German Defense League for People and Culture" (*Deutsche Schutzbund für Volk und Kultur*) [DSVK].[211] Overall these seem to be paper organizations of the DVU e.V. used to improve member statistics as well as produce new subscribers for Frey's publications and increase financial support and confirmation of his right-wing ideas. The *Aktiongemeinschaften* were formed to attract those who professed political stands which referred to subsections of right-wing extremism. These included those committees which had isolated viewpoints and undetectable radicalism.

One with such a profile, created in

---

[209] Mecklenburg (Hg.), Braune Gefahr, 24.
[210] Obszerninks and Schmidt, DVU im Aufwärtstrend, 16.
[211] Fischer, Ganz Rechts, 68.

November 1979, was the VOGA.[212] VOGA was founded to impose a statute of limitations on and a general amnesty for the crimes of National Socialists. The organization called for amnesty from what it perceived as a terror filled and conspicuous process of bringing cases to trial and the excessive length of time it took to prosecute a case. It also wanted changes because of the seeming general amnesty enjoyed by the victors for the more than nine million German civilians and soldiers it claimed had perished because of alleged Allied expulsion and starvation procedures between 1945 and 1950.[213] These *Aktiongemeinschaften* were organized so that someone with a particular interest became a member of an individual campaign community, was passed along to the DVU e.V, and automatically became a member of that organization. In December 1980, the Initiative for Foreign Delimitation (IFA) was created to keep the German character in Germany. It wanted the Germans of the Federal Republic to be unified with the Austrians and other middle European Germans to keep a German culture. VOGA called for taking back the cities from the foreign born and reported city populations had risen, with 25% being foreign born and 50% of all newborns born to foreign parents. By 1981 the ADRF announced its fight

---

[212] Obszerninks and Schmidt, DVU im Aufwärtstrend ,16.
[213] See James Bacque, *Crimes and Mercies: The Fate of German Civilians Under Allied Occupations, 1944-1950* (London: Little, Brown, and Company, 1997) and John Sack, *An Eye for an Eye: The Untold Story of Jewish Revenge Against Germans in 1945* (New York: Basic Books, 1993)

against the radical left-wing tendency in radio broadcasting and television.[214]

January 1982 found the ADRF protesting German television and its supposed disregard for German life and the rights of German people. The ADRF set itself against the disparaging view of Germany and German history and television's minimizing the loss of German civilian life during and after two world wars. During 1982 Frey befriended and encouraged British revisionist historian David Irving and supported Irving's denial concerning the Holocaust. Irving was a lecturer for the DVU e.V. a number of times and was repeatedly invited to club events. This revisionist perspective was capitalized on in January 1983 with the passing of Hans-Ulrich Rudel. The *Ehren Rudel Gemeinschaft* was created to protect the honor of the front-line soldier. Its members felt the reputation and honor of the German soldier and the military tradition of their fathers and grandfathers should be protected by law. Beyond this they held that the traditions and eternal values of German culture should be the focal point addressing the value of the historical models, experiences, and symbols. In addition, the *Ehren Rudel Gemeinschaft* called for former front-line soldiers, including the *Waffen-SS,* to be taken care of materially, and medal winners honored.[215]

By 1984 there was a move to defend the rights of citizens. In November 1984, the *Schutzbund für*

---

[214] Obszerninks and Schmidt, DVU im Aufwärtstrend, 17.
[215] *Ibid.*, 17,18.

Leben und Umwelt (Defense Association for Life and the Environment) was founded and pursued the goals of defending the unborn and protection of the environment. The association also called for the protection of citizens from the criminal element. In 1986 the action committee renamed itself the *Schutzbund für Volk und Kultur* (Defense Association for People and Culture). It became a non-partisan union of conscientious Germans with an interest in German people, language, and culture. All these action committees were under the financial and executive control of Gerhard Frey and his appointees.[216]

Frey, always looking to expand his publishing empire, purchased the *Deutsche Wochen-Zeitung* (DWZ) from its founder Waldemar Schütz, an NDP official in 1986. The paper had been in existence since 1958 but had suffered a decline in circulation. Eventually Frey restructured both the DWZ and DVU e.V.'s old club paper the *Deutsches Anzeiger* into a stronger *Deutsche Wochen-Zeitung*. This brought the circulation of Frey's publication empire, consisting of the *Deutsche Wochen-Zeitung* and *Deutsche National-Zeitung*, to over 55,000 copies, and by the end of the 1980s to one hundred thousand copies and eight to ten million marks. Because of Frey's chairmanship of the DVU e.V., his controlling influence over a half-dozen or more *Aktionsgemeinschaften*, and his influential membership in the NPD, these two newspapers were the voice of the right wing and various

---

[216] *Ibid.*

extremist elements of the right.[217]

Gerhard Frey had always declared that the DVU e.V. did not have plans to become a political party but was committed to be a collection point for conservative and nationalist thought and action. However, beginning in 1986 this sentiment started to change. Frey became bolder in his assertions about the failure of the Kohl government, the influx of foreigners and asylum seekers, and the problems of *Ostpolitik*. Frey felt it was time for the establishment of a new party. There had been several scandals within the government, the most damning being the Barschel-Pfeiffer Affair, which culminated in Barschel's death in 1987. Uwe Barschel (CDU), the state Prime Minister of *Schleswig-Holstein*, was accused of election machinations against the SPD candidate Björn Engholm. Pfeiffer was Barschel's media advisor and coconspirator in the action against the SPD. In addition to the political concerns there was a great deal of emotionalism concerning the problems of processing foreigners. Frey reasoned that a new party needed to form a coalition with existing parties or start off at zero. The party he had the most affinity with was the NPD. In March 1986 Frey as Chairman of the DVU e.V. and Martin Mußgnug as NPD chairman came to an agreement on a list of common candidates for the two parties. These contestants agreed to be sympathetic to each other and support each other. Frey established Germany's political alternative, the German List (Deutsche

---

[217] Fischer, *Ganz Rechts*, 27.

Liste), in November 1986 and announced its founding in the DNZ and the DWZ. The papers gave their support to various candidates on the federal list of nominees. In December, Frey renamed the Deutsche Liste with a name which held deep meanings from the past, the Deutsche Volksunion Liste D (DVU Liste D).[218]

On 5 March 1987, in the Munich *Lowenbräukeller* (Lion Brew Cellar), a group gathered that moved forward to stop the splintering of the right wing. National democrats, national liberalists, conservatives, and others met to set out in a new direction heading toward the revitalization of national unity and liberty of the whole German people. Another meeting took place on 2 April and resulted in an agreement between the president of the DVU Liste D and the NDP stating that the two parties would work together. The DVU Liste D took on the financial obligations of the change. There was an analysis of the various strengths and weaknesses on the regional level, with the understanding that neither party would run a candidate where the other was already running. The list of candidates between the two parties gave the appearance of a loose zipper. They were staggered geographically across the map, and yet they fit together to reach as many people as possible. Neither party broke its promise nor ran a candidate for the same office. The greatest advantage enjoyed was that each party would retain its own organizational self-sufficiency despite their

---

[218] Obszerninks and Schmidt, DVU im Aufwärtstrend, 19.

cooperation. The DVU Liste D gained little in the way of votes in 1987 and 1989.[219] However, DVU Liste D, having only 2,500 hundred members in 1987, did obtain 3.4% of the votes in the *Bremen Länder* elections, and by 1989 had grown to 25,000 members.[220] In 1989 Frey's party became involved in European politics, spending twenty million marks on publicity and campaigning for the European elections. Unfortunately for Frey, the result made little political impact as far as European politics were concerned. Frey, a businessman as well as a politician, remained the financial strength behind the party.[221] By 1990 Frey was getting discouraged, the NDP was doing poorly in the polls and had terrible election results, and the DVU Liste D had dropped to twenty-two thousand members. Frey still had victory in view and a dedication to a life duty.[222]

Post-Unification

Unification was the most important plank in the right-wing platform. When this plank was lost, the right had to scramble to find a suitable replacement. Right-wing strategy had to attract those who were opponents and victims of modernization and who saw their own status endangered.[223] It had to play

---

[219] Mecklenburg (Hg.), Braune Gefahr, 13.
[220] *Die Wel*t, 6 January 1999, 6.
[221] Fischer, *Ganz Rechts*, 69.
[222] Mecklenburg (Hg.), *Braune Gefahr,* 14. and *Die Welt*, 6 January 1999, 6.
[223] Uwe Backes, "Danger on the Right?" Internationale Politik

on the people's fear of losing their job, or their homes, and it aimed to profit from fears, prejudices, and resentments by exploiting social degeneration. This was difficult for the right because of Germany's peculiar politics. The Nazi past created constraints on openly mobilizing a right-wing electorate. These constraints include Germany's commitment to democracy, the 5% electoral law, and the constitutional court, which can outlaw political parties. In the former East Germany, right-wing extremism was not a phenomenon involving fringe groups or part of a sub-culture; it dominated the youth culture in many small villages and towns. The ideal eastern right-wing voter was typically a young male, with few denominational preferences, worried about losing his job and more highly educated than his western counterpart.[224] In the west, voter behavior was determined by the corrosion of the socio-cultural environment (rural village life, church communities, union organized labor, etc.), the loosening of party allegiances, and the shrinkage of the core voter groups of the established parties.[225] Although the CDU/CSU are particularly vulnerable to a loss of support due to the appeal of the radical right, none of the core

---

1 (Winter 2000), 56.

[224] Michael Miimkenberg, "What's Left of the Right," In Germany's New Politics: Parties and Issues in the 1990Õs, ed. David P. Conradt, Gerald R. Kleinfeld, George K. Romoser, and Chritian Søe, 255-271. (Providence: Berghahn Books, 1995), 264.

[225] Uwe Backes, "Danger on the Right?" 56.

parties are immune. [226] To gain voters the right capitalized on two resurgent issues, anti-Semitism, and the question of the eastern borders of Germany. These issues were fused with those which already made the right stand out, along with the question of immigration.[227]

To take advantage of the change in Germany's government and its political borders Frey wanted to transform the DVU from a club into a party. He foresaw positive impacts on the growth of the German right and to the DVU itself. Frey wanted a dissolution of the NDP by fusion with the DVU Liste D and constantly seeded the idea of the two parties uniting under his leadership. The NDP, however, was regionally a united structured organization which did not always agree with the DVU Liste D centralized organization. In addition, the youth organization of the NDP offered strong resistance to an alliance between the two. Frey wanted to draw as much personnel and party advantage as he could from his cooperation with the NPD. He pointed to the prominent role the DVU played in the alliance and how helpful it had been. Unfortunately, there was a glaring contradiction between the cooperation of the party officials and the abject distrust between the party bases.[228]

By 1991 the DVU Liste D had reversed its losses in membership and had climbed back up to

---

[226] Stephen Padgett, *Parties, and the Party Systems in the New Germany* (Brookfield, VT: Dartmouth Publishing Co., 1993), 93.
[227] Miimkenberg, What's Left of the Right, 266-268.
[228] Obszerninks and Schmidt, DVU im Aufwärtstrend, 20.

twenty-four thousand members. It had even won 6.2% of the vote in the Bremen election, jumping over the federally enacted 5% limit for participation in the government.[229] On 16 December 1991, at the large party rally in Passau, the cooperation between the NPD and the DVU Liste D was officially terminated. At the same rally the DVU Liste D amended its by-laws and changed its name to the *Deutsche Volksunion* (DVU).[230] Many saw this change in status between the NDP and Frey, and the change in name as no more than two parties going their separate ways. Others saw it as a reaction to the ascent of another right-wing party, the Republicans. The new rival REP surmised that it could have been Frey's dissatisfaction with the federal government, *Ostpolitik*, and the field of German politics.[231]

Frey and the DVU tried to gain right-wing support from every available source. Membership had risen to an all-time high of 26,000 in 1992 and 1993 and had achieved 6.3% of the vote in the 1992 *Schleswig-Holstein Länder* elections.[232] The DVU also cleared the 5% hurdle in *Baden-Württtemburg* with 10.9% of the vote.[233] With the increase for the DVU there was a corresponding decrease in the

---

[229] *Die Welt*, 6 January 1999, 6.
[230] Obszerninks and Schmidt, DVU im Aufwärtstrend, 20.
[231] Mecklenburg (Hg.), Braune Gefahr, 14.
[232] *Die Welt*, 6 January 1999, 6.
[233] Jonathan Carr, *Election Year 1994: Continuity and Change in the German Political Parties*, German Issues 15 (Washington, D.C.: American Institute for Contemporary German Studies, 1994), 21.

CDU's votes.[234] In 1993 the Russian right-wing leader Vladimir Volfovich Zhirinovsk was the guest of honor at the yearly grand party meeting in Passau. Frey returned the visit as the guest of Zhirinovsk and his liberal party in Moscow, where the two men pledged their support and friendship. By 1994 DVU membership had dropped to 20,000 and Frey was out to build political clout for his party and himself. He had a meeting with the 20,000-member REP party chairman Franz Schönhuber in August 1994, where the two laid their cards on the table and hashed through their differences. By the end of the meeting there was agreement on some basic principles of the right wing. Both felt there was a need to defend the right with a linked people's front as well as the different parties working together for common causes. Shortly after this meeting concluded, Schönhuber lost the chairmanship of the REP. Schönhuber's dismissal demonstrated there was just as much tension between the rank and file of the REP and DVU as there was between the NDP and the DVU. However, the REP did move farther to the right by exploiting anti-Semitic and revisionist views. Frey had greater control over the DVU, as was shown at the party conference, held at the *Nibelungenhalle* in Passau. The DVU pointed out the thousands who were attending and supporting the party conference. Frey praised the support of those who attended and

---

[234] Russell J. Dalton, *The New Germany Votes: Unification and the Creation of the New German Party System* (Providence: Berg Publishing, 1993), 240.

spoke on his standard theme of bogus asylum seekers, criminal foreigners, unemployment, pensions, social policies, and the Euro.[235]

The strongest of the right-wing parties in 1997 were the DVU and the REP. Both parties were at an all-time low in membership with 15,000-members each. Frey was coming under fire from within his own party. There were those who were against the almost autocratic organization of the party, which placed Frey and his family in significant and controlling roles. His wife and children were put in leadership and committee roles within the party and had the ability to control finances. Frey's personal empire began to be eyed as minor scandals and troubles began plagued him. At the same time, it was also recognized that Frey was a financial and real estate genius. While chairman of the party, he had made fortunes in his other endeavors. Frey's ambitions and talents ran in two directions: politics and business. He controlled eight million marks of the party's money and could decide how and why it was spent.[236]

Because of dissatisfaction with mainline parties, DVU's voter support began to grow again in 1998 with an increase of three thousand votes. In June 1998 Frey met with Jean-Marie LePen, leader of the French National Front. The REP had been both supporters and supported by the French National Front; however, in the middle of the 1990s the French National Front had started to change

---

[235] Mecklenburg (Hg.), Braune Gefahr, 15.
[236] Fischer, *Ganz Rechts*, 68-69.

direction. With the meeting in 1998 there was an agreement between the DVU and the French National Front.[237] This agreement, signed in Strasbourg, was a pledge for mutual support in the 1999 European Parliament election, and to combine efforts to fight the introduction of a single currency.[238] The *Deutsche National-Zeitung* wrote that Jean-Marie LePen had welcomed the recent success of the DVU and expressed his confidence that the party would leap forward in the *Bundestag*. Frey responded that the French National Front was the new model for the German right. In November 1998, a sudden meeting was arranged between Frey and REP chairman Rolf Schlierer. Afterwards it became apparent that an agreement had been made about the running of candidates in various election districts. The DVU did not have candidates in the *Hessen Länder* elections in February 1999 and beginning in June did not run any in the metropolitan council election. In a similar move the REP did without a candidate in the Bremen elections. An interlocking pattern began to appear, as it had previously with the NDP. Schlierer informed REP membership that the agreement with the DVU was an informal one. Attacking one another at the top of the party had to stop, and a common right-wing front was now necessary. Schlierer said in the REP paper Jungen Freiheit that now was the time for some manner of armistice.

---

[237] Mecklenburg (Hg.), Braune Gefahr, 16.
[238] Institute for Jewish Policy Research and American Jewish Committee, 1999. Germany.,
http://www.axt.org.uk/antisem/countries/germany.htm

Although Schlierer's predecessor Schönhuber had been dismissed four years earlier because of a similar stance, times had changed. The basic need was that all right-wing parties had to work together. Members of the DVU, NPD, and REP had to show unity at area levels. Schelierer felt that up to this time the REP had been following a rigid course which limited its dealings with other parties. The rivalry within the right wing had become futile and needed to be lifted out of the "brown" mire.[239] Frey further declared his willingness to harmonize the DVU cause at the national level even more closely with the REP, but a merger was not to be considered.[240]

Spring 1999 brought conflicts to the DVU. The parliamentary group of the *Landtag* of Saxon-Anhalt, which had numbered sixteen since April 1998, lost one of its members to the small right-extremist party *Vereinigte Rechte* (United Right) [VR]. Following further fierce squabbles in the autumn, which had been triggered chiefly by authoritarian leadership, the twelve-member parliamentary group reorganized itself. The autocratic leadership was also replaced, and one of the deputies who had left returned. In December 1999 two other deputies left over the decision not to run candidates in the *Schleswig-Holstein*

---

[239] Mecklenburg (Hg.), Braune Gefahr, 16.
[240] Budesrepublik Deutschland, *Bundesministerium des Innern. Annual Report of the Office for the Protection of the Constitution 1999* (Köln: Budesamt für Vefassungsschutz, 1999), 56.

elections.[241] Even with troubles the DVU remained the strongest of the right-wing extremist parties, with 17,000-members through 2000 and a circulation of between 45,000 and 50,000 copies per week of the *Deutsche National-Zeitung* and the *Deutsche Wochen-Zeitung*. The *Republikaner* party was the next largest party with 13.000-members and 20,000 copies in circulation of *Der Republikaner*. However, the REP had lost 1000 members between 1999 and 2000. During the same time the NPD rose from 6,000 to 6,500 members and kept the monthly circulation of the *Deutsche Stimme* at 10,000 copies.[242]

Two important aspects concerning the DVU can be gleaned from its history. One was a stable party membership over long periods of time despite public opinion and polling data. This stability occurred despite swings between conflict and collaboration of the DVU and other extreme right parties. However, Frey's attempts to add members through the party's special-cause organizations did not bear fruit either. DVU election results did swell periodically, but not because of increased membership. The swell was from right-wing voters

---

[241] *Ibid.*, 56-57.
[242] Budesrepublik Deutschland, *Bundesamt für Verfassungsschutz Presse – und Öffentlichkeitsarbeit. Rechtsextremismus in Deutschland - Ein Lagebild zu Beobachtungsschwerpunkten des Verfassungsschutzes* (Köln: Budesamt für Vefassungsschutz, 2000), 12-5. and Budesrepublik Deutschland, *Bundesamt für Verfassungsschutz Presse - und Öffentlichkeitsarbeit. Verfassungsschutzbreicht 2000* (Köln: Budesamt für Vefassungsschutz, 2001), 51-82.

of the main-stream parties supporting the DVU candidates. The DVU is evidence of the existence of a hard-core of right-wing extremist which were politically active. The party also provides a place for unhappy conservatives which are disillusioned by their own party.

Another aspect is that of Frey himself. Frey took a very active role in the politics and direction of the DVU. He, for the most part, financed the party; made most, if not all, of the important decisions; and had insured that he would remain in charge. Frey's wealth continued to give him an advantage in selection of committee members and those who would be supported politically and financially by the party. However, Frey was also a hindrance to the party. Although Frey was educated and well-read, he lacked the charisma and presence needed for a national leader. When he appears on "DVUTV - Das echte deutsche Fernsehen (DVU TV - Genuine German Television)," he would remind someone of a retired postman in a grey suit. His message was simple and his rhetoric predictable: asylum seekers, crime, foreigners, and German honor.

There were those with the opinion that the REP and the DVU had succeeded in moving the nation's political agenda to the right, especially on immigration and the status of foreigners within Germany.[243] Frey felt the central features of the right had remained the same. Not only did he use

---

[243] Gerard Brawnthal, *Parties and Politics in Modern Germany* (Bolder, Colorado: Westview Press, 1996), 190.

mass media, and political choreography but extreme right leadership principles such as xenophobia, radical nationalism and racism interspersed with Social Darwinism and mythological ideological elements.[244] Frey was able to lead the *Deutsch Volksunion* out of the twentieth century as the strongest financially and largest numerically extreme right-wing party in Germany with a publication department putting 50,000 papers into circulation a month. Gerhard Frey had built a party which put Germany and being German first.

---

[244] Michael G. Huelshott, *From Bundesrepublik to Deutschland: German Politics after Unification* (Ann Arbor: University of Michigan Press, 1993), 239.

Chapter 5
A Comparative Look at Anti-Semitism in the German People's Union and the Christian Social (Worker's) Party

Making a comparison between similar objects illuminates their uniqueness, and the same can be said of similar political parties. The DVU and the CSP/CSWP are two parties which are typically lumped together either as right-wing extremist parties or as some type of neo- or proto-Nazi organizations. They are seen as anti-Semitic, xenophobic and anti-democratic; however, in reality there are more differences than similarities. When analyzing the DVU and the CSP/CSWP five points of comparison will be examined. These areas include: the political landscape relative to each party, the party founder-leader, the party platform, the imagined other, and each party's similarity to Nazism.

The Political Landscape

It is important to review the political landscape for each of the political parties under examination. Surprisingly, the political outlook of the Christian Social (Worker's) Party and the German People's Union tend to run parallel but exhibit some noticeable differences.

Both parties operated within a relatively new parliamentary government. The CSP/CSWP was established seven years after the founding of the German Empire. Although there had been state parliaments with varied degrees of freedom and a North German Confederation, this was the first national German government. The constitution was borrowed from the North German Confederation, and the members of the *Reichstag* were elected by universal manhood suffrage. The government itself was autocratic, with the *Kaiser* irremovable. He was able to open and close sessions of the *Reichstag* and select the Chancellor. In addition, the imperial government could, through legislation, ban parties and drive their leaders underground. This does not mean that political parties did not have rights or made little impact on the governmental process, merely that their contribution to legislation was guided and at times controlled. The *Reichstag* did have power over the purse strings of the government and could control, within limits, expenditures for military and governmental budgeting. A strong Chancellor could bully the *Reichstag* as Bismarck did in the budget process of 1874.

The DVU was also established in a relatively new political system. After the Second World War, West Germany's political system was in a state of flux for a number of years, emerging finally as a federal republic. Right-wing parties were investigated for neo-fascist tendencies, and through the 1950's many were declared undemocratic and disbanded. The government, although a modern democracy, also exercised its power to disband parties through the Office for the Protection for the Constitution and drive their leaders underground. The legislature had devised a 5% rule, which limited party legislative representation to those who were able to achieve at least 5% of the overall vote.

Both parties suffered the vicissitudes of being part of the right wing. Support from membership was relatively small, financial support was shaky, and the party leadership tended to be authoritarian. In addition, both parties had to devise a number of alliances with rival parties which had similar party platforms, to further their own political objectives. The CSP/CSWP formed coalitions with the DKP and the Anti-Semitic league members, while the DVU had alliances with the NPD and the REP.

The major difference between the two political landscapes was their perceived inception. The CSP/CSWP was formed during a time of great national victory. The common outlook was positive, with the general population riding high from the Franco-Prussian war; everything seemed possible. However, it would be hard to ignore the economic slump 1873 had on the development the CSP/CSWP. It was the financial woes the poor and the working class were suffering that gave exigency to Stöcker's party. Much of what Stöcker saw when he directed the inner-city missions in Berlin motivated him to begin working politically. As the party grew and its membership composition moved from the working-class to the middle-class, which included craftsmen and merchants.

The DVU was founded after the worst defeat

the German nation had ever suffered. All of the government institutions had been destroyed, and the population tended to see themselves as European rather than German. Economically, the DVU was in a different situation. During the DVU's growth West Germany had general prosperity. Jobs were plentiful, and construction occurred throughout Germany. In East Germany, the communist government rebuilt the economy and infrastructure. Jobs in the east were available but they were not of the same quantity or quality as in the Federal Republic. This caused living conditions in the east to be more austere. The DVU, from its beginnings, enjoyed a fairly stable membership in West Germany, however, the communist government did not allow it in the East. After the unification, the DVU gained support from the new *Länder*. Many in the East became supporters of Frey's party because of its stand on foreigners, asylum seekers, and the federal government. This support came not only from the jobless and radical youth but from many who were fed up with the direction of the government and long for the stability of the past.

In general, the political landscape for the two parties were very similar. The differences included the mind-set of the population, the composition of the upper echelon of the executive branch of government, and the economies.

The Leader-Founder

Gerhard Frey and Adolf Stöcker have little in common in with each other. Frey, who founded the

DVU, was the son of an old, established, prominent business family. Born before the Second World War, Frey was a member of the Hitler Youth and grew up under the Nazi regime. When Germany lost the war, a lasting impression was made on Frey and his family. Frey saw the victorious powers entering the country and made a commitment that he would work toward the exoneration of Germany in general and the German army in particular. After the war, because of the family fortune, Frey was able to go to university and earn a Ph.D. in political science. He also inherited a fortune making him a multimillionaire and owner of a great deal of rental property in Berlin. In addition, he is co-owner with his brother, a major department store chain in Germany.

Stöcker, on the other hand, had a very different childhood and family background; his family was poor. Unlike Frey's father, Stöcker's father worked first as a blacksmith, later served in the military for 37 years, and finally became a prison guard in Prussia. Stöcker's parents had to sacrifice to put him through university for theology. His parents sacrifice was not forgotten by him and made an impression on him which surfaced later in life.

Stöcker and Frey's early styles of life were not their only differences. Their life after university was important in shaping their outlook on politics. Stöcker worked in a capacity which helped other people working first as a tutor for a number of years and later, utilizing his theology degree, became the pastor of a number of churches. He was called into service for the Franco-Prussian War and went to

Metz as a chaplain, later becoming divisional chaplain. During the war he saw the depths of human despair and countered it with rousing and patriotic sermons to the troops. His messages became known in imperial circles, and he was soon asked to be court chaplain. It was in Berlin that Stöcker became director of the city mission and saw the need of those on the streets and how they blamed the imperial government for their problems.

After Frey graduated from university, he vowed to restore the honor of Germany and the Nazis. He became employed by a right-wing newspaper owned and controlled by ex-Nazis. Frey used his money and connections to become a controlling partner and eventually buy the paper. During this time, he became more involved with various extreme right-wing parties including the NDP. He also bought other papers and expanded his publishing empire.

It is evident how these early years shaped Stöcker and Frey's political agenda. Stöcker became concerned with the plight of the poor and downtrodden and their view of the imperial government. He wanted to lift those who were down and out and to instill patriotism for the Emperor and Empire. Frey also wanted to see patriotism increase but in a different way. He was concerned with whitewashing the past and exonerating the Nazis.

Politics and Planks

The DVU and the CSP/CSWP had different foci on politics. The DVU's political thrust centered around retention of German identity, the refusal to renounce entitled German interest, equal rights for Germany on the world stage, protection from criminals, protection of pensions and social security benefits, the importance of the German citizen and help for middle class and farmers, direct democracy for German citizens, and a number of policies which deal with family and children, job creation, youth and education, and intensified environmental and animal protection.[245] There is another plank to the DVU platform which is not articulated in all of its literature or mentioned in an official capacity. This is the party's anti-foreigner plank. The party was against new immigration or the granting of citizenship to non-Germans living in the Federal Republic.

The CSP/CSWP platform was much simpler, with issues such as "professional corporations and compulsory arbitration, old age and invalid pensions, factory legislation, restoration of usury laws, progressive taxation, and taxation of stock exchange dealings and luxuries."[246] Also included in the CSP/CSWP plank was non-racial anti-Semitism. The party was not originally culturally anti-Semitic, however, as anti-Semitic elements drifted in the CSP/CSWP went in that direction.

Reviewing these party platforms illuminates the similarities between the two parties as well a

---

[245] *Deutsche Volksunion Partei - Programm* (München: Deutsche Vilksunion Verlag, 1999)
[246] P.G.J. Pulzer, *The Rise of Political Anti-Semitism in Germany and Austria* (New York: John Wiley & Sons Inc, 1964), 93.

number of differences. The resemblances center around the protection of pensions, social security benefits, and benefits for families. Both parties found it necessary to address the problems of workers such as the number of hours worked in a day, old age pensions, working conditions, and taxes. The parties are also found to be xenophobic to one degree or another. The DVU is more racially inclined than the CSP/CSWP, but both would fit under the xenophobe category.

Differences between the two parties are focused in some cases on nationalistic aspects, while others are merely cultural differences related to their era. Some of these topics overlap each other with aspects of both having a nationalistic and cultural flavor. Included in these differences are national identity, interest and equal rights for Germany, as well as topics such as policies dealing with the middle class and farmers, children, family, job creation, youth, and education.

On the surface these two parties look very similar; even their differences tend to be more cultural than political. Looking at their respective cultures and "reading between the lines" the subtle differences become more understandable. Stöcker and his party were concerned with two basic concepts. They wanted to lift people up economically and encourage them to be more patriotic. The CSP/CSWP encouraged people to remember the traditions of the past and be loyal to the empire and its leaders. It also wanted the aristocracy to lend a helping hand to those who were less fortunate. Stöcker believed in what the party stood for and the direction it was going in. His major objection to Judaism was not racial, but societal (religious) and economic. Overall, the CSP/CSWP wanted the imperial government to be involved with the welfare of its people and the people involved and supportive of the imperial government. However, this stance still was the basis of Nazi ideology, and for some ant-Semitism was racial during the Imperial period.

When closely examining the literature of the DVU only one conclusion can be drawn. Gerhard Frey and the DVU's major agenda was the re-creation of a National Socialist style of government and culture in Germany. It can certainly be seen that the DVU was concerned about the welfare of the German citizen and the German family and wanted programs for German youth. The only thing which the DVU appears more concerned about is the German nation and its status in the world community. The DVU was obsessed with Germany returning to its 1937 borders and having control over them. It wanted an end to open immigration and wanted those who do immigrate to Germany to be Germanized. The DVU also glamorizes the Second World War and the Third Reich. Frey's publishing house turned out videos and books which portray the Nazis society as normal. They included titles such as *Blitz Mädchen, Krieg in der Heimat*, or *Mama, was wollen diese Männer?*[247] and videos like *Geschichte der Hitler-Jugend,*

---

[247] *Blitz girls, War at Home, or Mom, What do These Men Want?*

Geschichte der Deutschen Luftwaffe, and *Feuersturm von Dresden.*[248] Even though the party did not openly portray itself as anti-Semitic, it published and promoted anti-Semitic literature. Examples of titles include *Jüdische Kriegserklärungen an Deutschland, Bilder die Fälschen: Dubliose Dokumenta zur Zeitgeschichte,* or *Jüdische Geschichte, Jüdische Religion: Der Einfluß von 3000 Jahren.*[249]

Even though the DVU and the CSP/CSWP appear to have a great many similarities there are actually some deep differences between the two. Their greatest difference involves their look at the "imagined other."

The Imagined Other

Benedict Anderson in his book *Imagined Communities*[250] tells us that the integrating potential of nationalism is contingent on a racialized and "imagined Other." The inconceivability of depicting this amazing concept of nationhood is intensified in racism; racism then becomes the prop which preserves an illusionary nationalist experience as the failure of national unity is

---

[248] *History of the Hitler Youth, History of the German Air Force,* and *Firestorm of Dresden*
[249] *Jewish Declarations of War on Germany, Pictures of the Forgeries: Doubtful Documents on Contemporary history,* or Jewish History, *Jewish Religion: The Influence of 3000 years.*
[250] Benedict Anderson, *Imagined Communities* (New York: Verso, 1983), 149-54.

projected on a racialized and imagined Other. Both the DVU and the CSP/CSWP utilized the idea of the "imagined Other" but in different ways.

The "imagined Other" for Stöcker and the CSP/CSWP were rich capitalistic Jews (a basic building block of Nazism). It needs to be remembered that when the party was first organized as the Christian Social Party, there was no "imagined Other." The goal of the party was to alleviate the plight of the poor and re-establish traditional values of God and country. However, this changed over time in subtle ways.

The birthplace of rich Jews as the "imagined other" was Jewish emancipation (1871). It was thought that rich Jews wanted to rid themselves of caring for their poorer brothers and sisters. By becoming emancipated, the poor Jews would have to be cared for by the government. This would free up Jewish capital for financial investments and for loans with usury. The perceived "rich Jews," along with non-Jewish Germans who deny their Christianity (a minority of the supposed total), began to be known as Semites. The term Semite was never intended by Stöcker to refer to Jews in a racial sense but in a capitalistic sense. It was assumed these Semites were making a great deal of profit and were becoming masters of the economy. Many thought that both individuals and governments were being controlled and under the "Jewish thumb."

The crash of 1873 and the woes of Germany were blamed on the "Semites" who it was believed had manipulated the market and the economy in such a way as to gain large profits and take greater control over the government. As the CSP/CSWP grew religious and cultural anti-Semitism became more prevalent. Stöcker and the party criticized the Jews, made anti-Semitic speeches, and wanted them to stay in their place, a type of second-class citizenship.

However, Stöcker, with a "pastor's heart" and a belief that because God loved the world and sent His Son for whosoever believed, felt that he should act just as forgiving. He deduced that upon conversion to Christianity a Semite (Jew) would no longer be an "imagined other" or a Semite but would have the rights of any other German. A straw position within the developing new paradigm.

Frey and the DVU had a different agenda and a different outlook on the "imagined other." The DVU had a scope larger and more encompassing. There are three "imagined others" in Frey's scenario; asylum seekers, foreigners (especially guest workers), and Jews. Each seen as keeping Germany from reaching its ultimate place in the world.

Asylum seekers were perceived by the DVU as a leech on the skin of the republic. The sequence of events was usually seen to include the asylum seekers entering Germany, fleeing terror and oppression in their home country. However, once entering, they never leave, even though the problems in their home country have been solved. By staying, they drain resources which are meant for German citizens and disrupt German cities with slums. Overall, they become a burden which could easily be rectified by expulsion.

Foreigners, especially guest workers, are another "imagined other." The DVU viewed them as a contamination to German society. They refuse to become acculturated and were believed to be a center of criminal activity. These foreigners who hold Germany back are not just those who come to the country but foreign governments as well. The British and Americans were seen as joining forces in an Anglo-American pact to keep Germany down and control its commerce. The European Union fit into this line of thinking by taking away the sovereign powers of Germany and replacing them with bureaucrats from other European countries.

Finally, the Jew is also seen as an "imagined other." It was not an official plank of the party; however, racial anti-Semitism was extremely interwoven in the DVU literature. Jews were considered foreign to German culture and society and as at the foundation of many of the problems in Germany today. Typically, it was not the number of Jews which was seen as a problem, although from the DVU's point of view any Jews were too many, because of the economic control they allegedly exercise over the country. The DVU insisted that the Jews were exploiting the Holocaust through 'lies" about what had happened and from reparations to which they were not entitled.

Although both parties have an "imagined other(s)" each party perceives their impacts in a slightly different manner. The CSP/CSWP did feel that the "Semites" were hurting Germany; however, there was a remedy for it. The remedy for the "imagined other" of the CSP/CSWP was baptism. With the DVU and its "imagined others" the only solution is expulsion in one form or another. Neither is an acceptable solution to an imagined problem.

Similarities to the Nazis

When looking at these two parties there is a need to compare them to the most extreme, anti-Semitic, and xenophobic of all right-wing parties in Germany, the Nazis. This comparison does not involve only a party and its programs but a regime and its deeds. Simply put, the Nazis were the proponents of racial and national discrimination. The idea was that anyone who was not of German or Aryan descent was unworthy of citizenship. There was no reprieve or redemption, if you did not measure up to Nazi standards then you were considered an enemy and an alien. However, it must be realized that you were German if the Nazis said you were German. Examples included *Luftwaffe Generalfeldmarshall* Erhard Milch who was vouched for by Göring or other officers such as General Helmut Wilberg, General Johannes Zuckertort, or Naval Commander Paul Ascher.

When reviewing the CSP/CSWP and the DVU in comparison to the Nazis, it is necessary to consider them within the context of their existence. The CSP/CSWP was founded fifty-five years before the Nazi takeover of Germany, and the DVU, as a party, was founded forty-two years after their demise. This is noteworthy since defeat in the Second World War had an impact upon the DVU which the CSP/CSWP did not have to contend with. Between the DVU and the CSP/CSWP, the DVU was more closely associated to the Nazis. The CSP/CSWP was certainly anti-Semitic and produced literature which was intended to expose "Semitic" plans and label them as such. However, Stöcker felt with conversion to Christianity this all would be changed; anyone who was baptized became welcomed and acceptable as a German citizen. Stöcker was abusive to the Jewish community who despised him for his use of degrading rhetoric. Stöcker, it seems had no idea of the depths anti-Semitism would reach.

The DVU, on the other hand knew exactly what the Nazi regime represented and the results it reaped. The DVU allowed for no provision such as conversion for 'redemption,' it wants the removal of the "imagined others" from German societies as did the Nazis. If the DVU came to power and was allowed to politically carry out its platform, there would be numerous similarities to the Nazis. Foreigners would be expelled almost immediately, and Jews would be hampered economically, if not relegated outright to second class citizenship. The government would be centralized, and individual state powers would be redistributed between state and federal components.

Another expectation of the DVU in power was expansionist tendencies. One can almost hear Frey demanding parts of the former eastern territories back from Russia and Poland much as Hitler did from Czechoslovakia and Poland. The DVU preached pacifist ideology and at times even proclaimed that it would not want any part of the former German Reich if acquisition was by violent methods. DVU rhetoric, however, typically urged Germans to not forget those who were violently expelled from Germany's eastern provinces and the urgency to have these provinces returned.

Synopsis

Knowledge of the two parties reveals many similarities. Their official planks and platform sentiments were comparable, and in some cases, they appeared to be moving in the same or parallel circles. They both professed concern for the working class as well as merchants and farmers. Yet, when the differences are explored and delineated, it is clear that these parties are not identical.

The differences between the two parties is exposed in the focus of their leaders' objectives. Stöcker's objective was to improve the lot of the poor through the interaction of the church and the government. He saw this change through the Christian Baptism of Jews and non-believers feeling that this would reinvigorate the economy and national sentiment.

Frey's theme centered upon the restoration and recovery of that which was confiscated or lost by the German *Volk* and a recapturing of German superiority in the world. This included foreigners and those who were both/either religious and/or culturally Jewish.

Chapter 6
Encapsulation

Over time German legal and political theory has stressed the duties of the individual in relation to the state rather than state responsibility toward the protection of individual liberties. German political thinkers define liberty as the individual having freedom only within the confines of the state, with compliance to the state's laws and statutes the only way to secure one's freedom and personal improvement.[251] This attitude has enabled the periodic resurgence of the right-wing with the extreme right rearing up and subsiding throughout German history.[252] Surprisingly many act as though right-wing extremists were a unique example in an otherwise flawless society. Looking closer at the problems in mainstream German society reveal that the cause of extremism lies in their ideology of freedom.[253] This can be said of both the German People's Union and the Christian Social (Worker's)

---

[251] David P. Conradt, *The German Polity*, (New York: Longman, 1989), 59. and Matthew Levinger, *Enlightened Nationalism: The Transformation of the Prussian Political Culture* (New York: Oxford University Press, 2000), 5.
[252] Jonathan Carr, *Election Year 1994: Continuity and Change in the German Political Parties, German Issues 15* (Washington, D.C.: American Institute for Contemporary German Studies, 1994), 20.
[253] Wilhelm Heitmeyer, "Selbsttäuschung: Rechts kommt nicht aus dem Nichts," Kulturchronik 2000 18, Nr. 6 (2000), 22.

Party. Both were a reaction to the society in which they found themselves. The CSP/CSWP was a reaction to the needs of the poor, the loss of traditions in society, and the threat of unrestrained predatory capitalism.

The DVU, on the other hand, was a reaction to the loss of the Second World War, the toppling of the Nazi government, and the loss of international prestige and economic power. In addition, the DVU wanted to right the wrongs of the past and revise the history of the Nazi party, whitewashing Nazi deeds during the war. The DVU's reaction is similar to that of the Nazi party after the signing of the Treaty of Versailles after the First World War.

The Nazi Party was a reaction to the Treaty of Versailles and the loss of German pride and international power. It, too, tried to revise the past by blaming the Jews and Communist for the defeat in the War, the loss of the monarchy, and the humiliation of the military forces at home and in the field. Both the DVU and the Nazis used similar methods of propaganda and intimidation, although of different intensities. The DVU could not match the Nazis in ferocity because of the influence of the conquering powers of the Second World War and the limits put on them by the German constitution.

When we look at the DVU, it becomes apparent that its ideology was different than that of the CSP/CSWP and was really closer to that of the Nazi party of the 1930s and 1940s. The DVU was xenophobic, anti-Semitic, and anti-democratic, and had many of the same planks as was found in original twenty-five points of the Nazi platform. In fact, its anti-democratic stance was not just part of the national platform but can be traced to the political workings of the party itself.

When considering the Nazi party, Adolf Hitler not only was the absolute leader of Germany but also the party. Although legally accomplished, the Nazi regime perverted the constitutional government of the German (Weimar) Republic, reorganizing it into a dictatorship. Moreover, Hitler hijacked Anton Drexler's German Worker's Party in 1920 and turned it into the National Socialist German Workers Party. This is also true with the DVU party hierarchy; Gerhard Frey was the absolute leader. He controlled its leadership and had underwritten a large part of its finances, keeping himself and his cronies in complete control. In regard to national leadership, the DVU wanted a nationally elected leader as opposed to the current prime minister/chancellor chosen from parliament. It believed that the German people were not able to speak out with a clear enough voice through the *Bundestag* and needed someone who is elected directly by them.

Unlike the Nazis and the DVU, the CSP/CSWP supported the government in power wanting only to strengthen and expand it. Stöcker was loyal to the crown and envisioned the *Kaiser* and aristocracy taking care of the poor, guiding the country, and protecting those who were less fortunate. Stöcker never talked of overthrowing the government or forcing the *Kaiser* to abdicate. Hitler, on the other hand, tried to topple the Weimar government with the failed Beer Hall Putsch. Frey had not attempted a direct confrontation with the Federal Republic's government, however; he had unofficially tried to incite violence in different localities using the youth.

There is another factor involved when looking at the DVU and the CSP/CSWP. The DVU is well aware of the Nazi past and yet opted to emulate it in many ways. When reviewing the history of right-wing parties those which were conceived after 1945 had Nazi tendencies such as the REP, NPD, DVU, and similar parties tend to be extremist and xenophobic. Stöcker's party had a different dimension to their politics; the DVU had influences which were not conceivable to the Christian Social (Worker's) Party.

Although the Christian Social (Worker's) Party was anti-Semitic, it was certainly not of the same level or rank as the German People's Union or the Nazis. A closer look at the DVU reveals that this party more closely resembles the Nazis of the 1930s and 1940s than does Stöcker's party.

However, that is not to say that some forms of anti-Semitism (or racism in general) is benign or that there weren't any murders, rapes and prejudicial treatment during the Imperial period, rather a notorious ideology can become even more deadly when socio-economic situations are influx and a large number of "haves" become "have nots."

Once anti-Semitism became acceptable and tolerable during the Imperial period; developed into a violent and jingoistic ideology during the Nazi period it became endemically acceptable and enduring in German society in the Federal period.

This is what we see in Germany. Once society became tolerable of violent murderous prejudicial anti-Semitism it stayed acceptable to large portions of society and in some *Länder* became politically viable late into the 20th century.

Literature Review of Sources

While surveying the sources for this book very few were found written in English that addressed Gerhard Frey, Adolf Stöcker or the history of either the DVU or the CSP/CSWP. There were numerous German language publications that discuss different aspects of the DVU and CSP/CSWP.

Books regarding Adolf Stöcker and his party included works such as Grit Koch's *Adolf Stöcker, 1835-1909: ein Leben zwischen Politik und Kirche*, which deals with the life of Stöcker in the ministry from chaplain in the military to service as court chaplain for the Kaiser. Further, it considers the tension in his life between the church and politics as well as Christianity and the drives of the anti-Semitic forces at work in Germany in the latter half of the 19th century. *Protestantismus und Politik: Werk und Wirkung Adolf Stöcker* by Günter Brakelmann is another work which views this tension between the church and politics. Two other books are *Kirche am Abgrund: Adolf Stöcker und seine antijüdische Bewegung* by Hans Engelmann and *Hofprediger Adolf Stöcker und die chrislich-soziale Bewegung* by Walter Frank. These books contemplate the political and anti-Semitic side of Stöcker; however, they deal with the religious factors in his life. Frank's book, published during the Third Reich, contributed information and facts to P.J. Pulzer work, *The Rise and Fall of Political Anti-Semitism in Germany and Austria*.

German publishers have produced a number of books on Gerhard Frey and the DVU. These include *DVU im Aufwärtstrend-Gefahr für die Demokratie? Fakten, Analysen, Gegenstrategien* by Britta Obszerninks and Matthias Schmidt. This work deals with facts, analysis and opposition strategy of the DVU and the danger it presents to democracy. A similar book to this is *Der Multimillionär und die DVU: Daten, fakten, Hintergründe*, by Annette Link, focusing on Frey, his life, his control over the party and the party itself. Another German publication which deals with the DVU and Frey is *Braune Gefahr: DVU, NPD, REP, Geschichte und Zukuft* that is edited by Jens Mecklenburg. Although Mecklenburg's book deals with the DVU it also discusses the NPD and REP.

Primary Sources of the Study

Primary sources for this study came from three different areas. Two of these were publications by the *Deutsche Volksunion* and the *Bundesrepublik Deutschalnd*. The other primary source is a book written by a past member of the DVU.

The DVU documents used comprise:

<u>Aktion Oder-Neiße</u>: A non-partisan program is described which proclaimed the right of the German nation to be culturally German, united, with equal rights on the world stage and the undeniability of the German territory east of the Oder-Neiße line.

Deutsche National-Zeitung; Deutsche Wochen-Zeitung; Deutsche Anzeiger: Newspapers published by the DVU. They were a mix of party news, editorials, and book advertisements and were used in this study to illuminate the xenophobic and anti-Semitic aspects of the party's personality.

Deutsche Volksunion Partei-Programm: This document describes the basic party platform of the DVU. It was a compilation of various political stands such as German identity and national rights, youth, education, job creation, protection from criminals, and centralized direct democracy.

Initiative für Ausländer-Begrenzung: The details of this source illuminate the DVU's desire to limit foreign encroachment on German culture. It called for limits on immigration and the return to Germany of its hereditary lands and control over them.

Jung, Deutsch, Deutlich: A pamphlet outlining what the DVU wanted to achieve for the youth of Germany. It talks about Germany supporting German youth first and creating and safeguarding training and education opportunities. The pamphlet also pointed to multiculturalism as destroying society.

Letters from Deutscher Buchdienst: A series of letters between the author of this study and Dr. Gerhard Frey's *Deutscher Buchdiesnt* between 2 March 2000 and 1 March 2002. The letters are Frey's personal appeal (each letter signed by Frey) to buy a number of different books published by his publishing house. Typical titles advertised include *Die Holocaust-Industrie*; *Jüdischer Geschichte, Jüdische Religion*; *Deutsche Soldaten - Mörder oder Helden*; and *Jüdische Kriegserklärungen an Deutschland*.

Our Aims and Principal Policies: This English website was the home page of the Berlin office of the DVU. It dealt KTVB Live with the platform, principles, and ideals of the party. Although very similar to Deutsche Volksunion Partei-Programm, it presented this information with a different emphasis, which is friendlier and politically correct.

The *Bundesrepublik* primary literature used for this investigation included:

Annual Report of the Office for the Protection of the Constitution 1999: This report is similar to the Federal Ministry of the Interior Annual Report 1998. It deals with many of the same issues and stances of the DVU, NPD, and the REP for the year 1999.

Federal Ministry of the Interior Annual Report 1998: The 1998 report of right- and left-extremist endeavors. The paper presents an overview of the right-wing and then looks at violence and the neo-Nazi aspects of extremism. It then investigates the DVU, NPD, and REP. A similar treatment of left-wing extremism is also provided.

Rechtsextremismus in Deutschland: Ein Lagebild zu Beoactungsschwer-punkten der Vefassungsschutzes: This booklet investigates the background of right-wing violence. It looks at the structure of the violence, what is proven or suspected, neo-Nazism, and the roots to the threat of terrorism. A look at the three major right-wing extremist parties (DVU, NPD, and REP) is also included.

Rechtsextrenistische Parteien in der Bundesrepublik Deutschland - Agitation, Ziele, Wahlen: This 1999 publication relates information on the three major extremist parties in Germany: the German People's Union; the Republican Party; and the National Democratic Party of Germany. Each party is reviewed with regard to their stance on immigrants, anti-Semitism, democratic principles, the relevance of the atrocities of the Third Reich, and their ability to obtain votes.

Right-wing Extremism in Germany: This article published by the German federal government deals with the situation in 2001 with right-wing extremism. Its emphasis is on the main activities of the authorities responsible for protecting the German constitution against those who are extremist and anti-democratic.

Trends in the Right -Wing Extremism in the New Federal States: The new German states in the East have a unique situation with right-wing extremism. This pamphlet, printed in 2000, details the overall situation in the East and warns of the latent power the extreme elements of the electorate have.

Verfassungsschutzbericht 2000: A report which begins with some basic facts about the situation and a frank discussion of the constitution and democracy. The report then is broken down into two sub-sections, the Efforts of the Extremist Right and the Efforts of the Extremist Left. The section on the extreme right discusses their ideology and development. Subsequent sections look at organization and personnel, the background of the movement and how it is poised as a ready force for violence. The three major right extremist parties are studied. Each one's organization and development along with their youth movement are examined. A similar review is done for the extreme left.

A further primary source used was the book *Ganz rechts: Mein Leben in der DVU*. This is an autobiographical account of Jörg Fischer's life and his function in the DVU. He describes how he joined, attended party rallies, and worked for the party. In addition, he provides an overview of the DVU's history, parliamentary procedures, and a candid look from the inside.

Significant Secondary Sources of the Study

A number of secondary sources were of significant help to the study. These works do not incorporate all of the sources consulted but those which contributed a great deal of information to the study. These included:

A History of Modern Germany 1840-1945 by Hajo Holborn: A book which details the history of Germany and covers pertinent history dealing with the CSP/CSWP and anti-Semitism. It also gives an in-depth overview of the right-wing in Germany and the dynamics involved.

Basic Law for the Federal Republic of Germany (Grundgesetz): The constitution, ratified by all states, of the new unified Federal Republic of Germany.

Braune Gefahr: DVU, NPD, REP, Geschichte und Zukuft edited by Jens Mecklenburg: As the title suggests the book looks at the history, future and neo-Nazi danger of the three extremist parties DVU, NPD, and REP. The portion of the book which treats the DVU includes its history, the history of the multimillionaire Gerhard Frey, and the organization and function of his press.

DVU im Aufwärtstrend-Gefahr für die Demokratie? Fakten, Analysen, Gegenstrategien by Britta Obszerninks and Matthias Schmidt: This monograph deals with facts, analysis and opposition strategy of the DVU and the danger it presents to democracy. Topics covered in the book range from a short history of the DVU, to its lack of organization, new formations in the extreme right, and the strongholds of the DVU in Bremen, Schleswig-Holstein and Hamburg. It also investigates the leadership strength of the DVU in the extremist camp and its danger to democracy.

German Nationalism: The Tragedy of a People by Louis L. Snyder: A work which contains an overview of German nationalism and reasons for the rise of Nazism. In particular he has a section on religion which looks at Stöcker, the German national soul, and anti-Semitism.

Germany 1870-1945: Politics, State Formation, and War by P.J. Pulzer: This work explores the road to unity for the German people and the attempts to build a nation state. It begins with the Bismarck's Empire and continues through the Wilhelmine Empire, the First World War and revolution, the Weimar Republic and ends with the Third Reich.

Parties and Politics in Modern Germany - by Gerard Braunthal: Braunthal's book is broken down into four major sections. Each section reviews the modern parties of Germany in different ways. He gives an international and national overview of German politics. He then goes on to inspect the parties in both West and East Germany and then looks at the various parties after the unification of Germany. Important to this paper were those sections concerning right-wing parties and the parties in East Germany.

The Rise and Fall of Political Anti-Semitism in Germany and Austria by P.J. Pulzer: Pulzer's work begins with an overview of the Jews and their environment and the structure of society in Germany and Austria. He deals with the rejection of liberalism and then begins an extensive look at Germany and Austria between 1867 and 1900. For this study, Pulzer's book contains information concerning the CPS/CPWS and the Berlin movement. He also deals with the problems of anti-Semitism and the changing role of the conservative party.

Wilhelm Marr-The Patriarch of Anti-Semitism by Moshe Zimmerman: This work is the biography of Wilhelm Marr who was the first to coin the phrase "anti-Semitism." Marr was a true anti-Semite both racially and religiously who was additionally anti-Christian. The work contains a great deal of information about Stöcker and the CSP/CSWP, as well as about de Grousillier.

Bibliography

Backes, Uwe. "Danger on the Right?" *Internationale Politik* 1 (Winter 2000): 53 - 61.

Brawnthal, Gerard. *Parties and Politics in Modern Germany*. Boulder, Co Älorado: Westview Press, 1996.

Bundesrepublik Deutschland, *Bundesamt für Verfassungsschutz Presse – und Öffentlichkeitsarbeit. Verfassungsschutzbreicht 2000*. Köln: Budesamt für Vefassungsschutz, 2001.

_____. *Rechtsextremismus in Deutschland - Ein Lagebild zu Beobachtungsschwerpunkten des Verfassungsschutzes*. Köln: Budesamt für Vefassungsschutz, 2000.

_____. *Rechtsextremismus Parteien in der. Budesrepublik Deutschland - Agitation, Ziele, Wahlen*. Köln: Budesamt für Vefassungsschutz, 1999.

_____. *Federal Ministry of the Interior Annual Report for 1998*. Köln: Budesamt für Vefassungsschutz, 1999.

_____. *Right-wing Extremism in Germany*. Köln: Budesamt für Vefassungsschutz, 2001.

_____. *Bundesministerium des Innern. Annual Report of the Office for the Protection of the Constitution 1999*. Köln: Budesamt für Vefassungsschutz, 1999.

_____. *Federal Office for the Protection of the Constitution. Trends in Right-Wing Extremism in the New Federal States*. Köln: Bundesamt für Vefassungsschutz, 2000.

_____. *Federal Ministry of the Interior, Press Section. Report for the Year 2000 on the Protection of the Constitution*. Köln: Bundesamt für Vefassungsschutz, 2001

Carr, Jonathan. *Election Year 1994: Continuity and Change in the German Political Parties*. German Issues 15. Washington, D.C.: American Institute for Contemporary German Studies, 1994.

Conradt, David P. *The German Polity*. New York: Longman, 1989.

Dalton, Russell J. *The New Germany Votes: Unification and the Creation of the New German Party System*. Providence: Berg Publishing, 1993.

Deutsche Volksunion. *Deutsche Volksunion Partei - Programm*. München: Deutsche Volksunion Verlag, 1999

_____. *Initiative für Ausländer - Begrenzung*. München: DSZ - Verlag GmbH., 1999

Fischer, Jörg. Ganz *Rechts: Mein Leben in der DVU. Reinbek bei Hamburg: Rowolt Taschenbuch* Verlag Gmbh, 1999.

Gellately, Robert. *The Politics of Economic Despair: Shopkeepers and German Politics 1890-1914*. Beverly Hills: SAGE Publications, 1974.

Heitmeyer, Wilhelm. "Selbsttäuschung: Rechts kommt nicht aus dem Nichts." *Kulturchronik 2000* 18, Nr. 6 (2000): 21 - 23.

Holborn, Hajo. *A History of Modern Germany 1840 - 1945*. Princeton: Princeton University Press, 1969.

Huelshott, Michael G. *From Bundesrepublik to Deutschland: German Politics after Unification*. Ann Arbor: University of Michigan Press, 1993.

Institute for Jewish Policy Research and American Jewish Committee, 1999. *Germany*., http://www.axt.org.uk/antisem/countries/germany.htm

Kahlund, Marco. "DVU und Republikaner - zwei rechtsextreme Parteien im deutsche Parteiensystem." *Staatsprüfung für die Laufban der Realschullehrer*, Schleswig-Holstein, 1999.

Kauders, Anthony. *German Politics and the Jews: Düsseldorf and Nuremberg 1910-1933*. Oxford: Clarendon Press, 1996.

Langewiesche, Dieter. *Liberalismus in Deutschland*. Frankfurt am Main: Suhrkamp Verlag, 1988.

Levinger, Matthew. *Enlightened Nationalism: The Transformation of the Prussian Political Culture*. New York: Oxford University Press, 2000.

Levy, Richard S. *The Downfall of the Anti-Semitic Political Parties in Imperial Germany*. New Haven: Yale University Press, 1975.

Link, Annette. *Der Multimillionär und die DVU: Daten, Fakten, Hintergründer*. Essen: Klartext-Vlg., 1994

Mecklenburg (Hg.), Jens. Braune *Gefahr: DVU, NPD, REP. Geschichte und Zukunft*. Berlin: Elefanten Press, 2001.

Miimkenberg, Michael. "What's Left of the Right," In Germany's *New Politics: Parties and Issues in the 1990's*, ed. David P. Conradt, Gerald R. Kleinfeld, George K. Romoser, and Chritian Søe, 255-271. Providence: Berghahn Books, 1995.

Müller, Jan - Werner. *Another Country: German Intellectuals, Unification, Hand National*

Identity. New Haven: Yale University Press, 2000.

Nagle, John D. *The National Democratic Party: Party Radicalism, in the Federal Republic of Germany*. Berkeley: University of California Press, 1970.

Nichols, A.J. *Weimar and the Rise of Hitler*. Glasgow: The University Press Glasgow, 1968.

Nichols, J. Alden. *Germany after Bismarck: The Caprivi Era 1890-1894*. Cambridge, MA: Harvard University Press, 1958.

Obszerninks, Britta and Matthias Schmidt. *DVU im Aufwärtstrend - Gefahr für die Demokratiec? Fakten, Analysen, Gegenstrategien*. Münster: Agenda Verlag, 1998.

Our Aims and Principal Policies. Berlin: www.DVU.net/Berlin.htm, 2000.

Padgett, Stephen. *Parties and the Party Systems in the New Germany*, Brookfield, VT: Dartmonth Publishing Co., 1993.

Prowe, Diethelm. "Prospects for the New Germany: Reading the Historical Evidence 1945-1960 and 1989 - 1991." *The Historian* 54 (Autumn, 1991): 19 - 35.

Pulzer, P.G.J. *The Rise of Political Anti-Semitism in Germany and Austria*. New York: John Wiley & Sons Inc, 1964.

_____. *Germany 1870-1945: Politics, State Formation, and War*. New York: Oxford University Press, 1997.

"Rechtsextreme Kandidaten mit Profil," *Der Spiegel*, 7 September 1998, 48.

Roberts, Geoffrey K. *Party Politics in the New Germany*, Washington: Pinter, 1997.

Rohe, Karl. Elections, *Parties and Political Traditions: Social Foundations of German Parties and Party Systems, 1867-1987.* New York: Berg Publishing, 1990.

Rosenberg, Arthur. *The Birth of the German Republic 1871-1918*. New York: Russell & Russell, 1962.

Schümer, Dirk. "Europa und die Fremdenfeindlichkeit: Wir geben nichts!" *Kulturchronik 2001* 19, Nr. 3 (2001): 20 - 22.

Shaikh, Mohammad A. "Germany Leads New Tide of Racism and Xenophobia Sweeping Europe," *Muslimedia,* 16-31 May 1998, Muslimedia.com.

Snyder, Louis L. *German Nationalism: The Tragedy of a People, Extremism Contra Liberalism in Modern German History*. Harrisburg: The Stockpole Company, 1952.

Staud, Toralf. "Fremdenfeindlichkeit bliebt zu oft unwidersprochen: Courage - ein Schul Projeckt in Sachsen." *Kulturchronik 2000* 18, Nr. 5 (2000): 18 - 20.

_____. "Rechtsradikalismus: Der Ostern ist brauner als es viele Politiker wahrhaben wollen." *Kulturchronik 2001* 19, Nr. 2 (2001): 19.

Steven Roth Institute for the Study of Contemporary Anti-Semitism and Race, *Project for the Study of Anti-Semitism: Germany 1998-1999*, Tel Aviv University, http://www.tau.ac.irl/anti-semitism/Institute.html

"Tabelle," *Die Welt*, 6 January 1999, 6.

Ulm, Ebner, ed. *Basic Law for the Federal Republic of Germany*. Berlin: German Bundestag Administration, Public Relations Section, 2001.

U.S. Department of the Army. *U.S. Army Area Handbook for Germany, Foreign Areas Studies Division: Special Operations Research*, Washington D.C., 1964.

van den Brink, Rinke. "Ohne Führer kein Erfolg?" *taz - LeMonde diplomatique*, 15 December 1995, 7.

Veen, Hans-Joachim, Norbert Lepszy and Peter Mnich. *The Republikaner Party in Germany: Right-*

Wing Menace or Protest Catchall? Westport: Praeger, 1993.

Volkov, Shulamit. *The Rise of Popular Anti-Modernism in Germany: The Urban Master Artisans, 1873-1896*. Princeton: Princeton Universitëy Press, 1978

Wallace, Charles P. "Angry Voters Turn to the Right," *Time International*, 20 September 1999, 43.

Wank, Ulrich. *The Resurgence of Right-Wing Radicalism in Germany: New Forms of an Old Phenomenon?* New Jersey: Humanities Press, 1993.

Wetzel, Bruno. *Aktion Oder-Neiße Programm*. München: DSZ-Verlag, 1999.

"Würstchen ohne Senf," *Der Spiegel*, 7 September 1998, 48.

Zimmermann, Moshe. *Wilhelm Marr: The Patriarch of Anti-Semitism*. New York: Oxford University Press, 1986.

www.ingramcontent.com/pod-product-compliance
Lightning Source LLC
Chambersburg PA
CBHW051834090426
42736CB00011B/1805